JUSTICE AGAINST SPONSORS OF TERRORISM ACT

HEARING

BEFORE THE

SUBCOMMITTEE ON THE CONSTITUTION
AND CIVIL JUSTICE

OF THE

COMMITTEE ON THE JUDICIARY
HOUSE OF REPRESENTATIVES

ONE HUNDRED FOURTEENTH CONGRESS

SECOND SESSION

ON

H.R. 2040

JULY 14, 2016

Serial No. 114–87

Printed for the use of the Committee on the Judiciary

$$\complement$$

Available via the World Wide Web: http://judiciary.house.gov

U.S. GOVERNMENT PUBLISHING OFFICE

20–724 PDF   WASHINGTON : 2016

For sale by the Superintendent of Documents, U.S. Government Publishing Office
Internet: bookstore.gpo.gov   Phone: toll free (866) 512–1800; DC area (202) 512–1800
Fax: (202) 512–2104   Mail: Stop IDCC, Washington, DC 20402–0001

COMMITTEE ON THE JUDICIARY

CONTENTS

JULY 14, 2016

Page

THE BILL

OPENING STATEMENTS

WITNESSES

JUSTICE AGAINST SPONSORS OF TERRORISM ACT

THURSDAY, JULY 14, 2016

House of Representatives

Subcommittee on the Constitution
and Civil Justice

Committee on the Judiciary

Washington, DC.

The Subcommittee met, pursuant to call, at 10 a.m., in room 2237, Rayburn House Office Building, the Honorable Trent Franks, (Chairman of the Subcommittee) presiding.

Present: Representatives Franks, DeSantis, Goodlatte, Jordan, Cohen, Conyers, Nadler, and Deutch.

Staff Present: (Majority) Zachary Somers, Parliamentarian & Chief Counsel, Committee on the Judiciary; Tricia White, Clerk; (Minority) James Park, Chief Counsel; Susan Jensen, Senior Counsel; Matthew Morgan, Professional Staff Member; and Veronica Eligan, Professional Staff Member.

Mr. FRANKS. The Subcommittee on the Constitution and Civil Justice will come to order, and without objection, the Chair is authorized to declare a recess of the Committee at any time. Welcome to all of you here. The subject of today's hearing is the Senate-passed version of the Justice Against Sponsors of Terrorism Act, or JASTA for short. Earlier this year, this legislation was unanimously reported out of the Senate Judiciary Committee, and in May, passed the Senate by a voice vote.

However, despite the broad bipartisan support for this legislation in the Senate, the State Department has raised concerns with JASTA, and we have called this hearing to examine those concerns. JASTA essentially makes two changes to Federal law.

First, it amends the Foreign Service Immunities Act to add the existing exceptions to the foreign sovereign immunity and exception for terrorist attacks that cause physical injury or death in the United States. Under current law, there appears to be some confusion or disagreement in the courts as the whether the Foreign Sovereign Immunity Acts tort exception waives the immunity of foreign governments that provide material support to foreign terrorist organizations that cause damage in the United States.

JASTA makes clear that a foreign government that aids and abets a foreign terrorist organization in carrying out a terrorist at-

(1)

tack on U.S. soil will not be immune from the jurisdiction of our court.

Second, JASTA amends the Antiterrorism Act to clarify that those who aid, abet, or conspire with a foreign terrorist organization are subject to civil liability. There is currently a split in the Federal Courts of Appeal on the question of whether the Antiterrorism Act permits lawsuits based on aiding and abetting terrorists.

JASTA provides that if a person aids and abets a State Department-designated foreign terrorist organization by knowingly providing that organization with substantial assistance, that person will be subjected to civil liability.

By making these two changes to existing law, JASTA seeks to ensure that those, including foreign governments, who sponsor terrorist attacks on U.S. soil are held fully accountable for their actions. In addition, JASTA attempts to enhance the effectiveness of U.S. efforts at combatting terrorism and combatting terrorist financing by making those who provide financial support to foreign terrorist organizations liable for their conduct.

JASTA would appear to be consistent with existing U.S. principles of foreign sovereign immunity, which permits lawsuits against foreign governments in U.S. court cases in the following instances—in which a foreign government has waived its immunity, that are based on a commercial activity carried out in the United States or which causes a direct effect in the United States, or in which the rights and property taken in violation of international laws are at issue, or in which money damages are sought against a foreign state for personal injury or death, or damage or loss of property occurring in the United States, and finally that are brought against designated state sponsors of terrorism.

Despite the numerous, longstanding exceptions to foreign sovereign immunity already provided under U.S. law, the State Department and others have expressed concerns with JASTA and its potential ramifications on U.S. foreign policy. Out of respect for those concerns, we have invited the State Department here to testify before the Committee, and we have also invited a second panel of witnesses to appear and provide additional perspective on the issues the State Department has raised with JASTA.

I look forward to the witnesses' testimony on this important subject, and I would now recognize the Ranking Member of the Subcommittee, Mr. Cohen, for his opening statement.

[The bill, S. 2040, follows:]

IC

114TH CONGRESS
2D SESSION

S. 2040

IN THE HOUSE OF REPRESENTATIVES

MAY 17, 2016

Referred to the Committee on the Judiciary

AN ACT

To deter terrorism, provide justice for victims, and for other purposes.

1   *Be it enacted by the Senate and House of Representa-*

2 *tives of the United States of America in Congress assembled,*

1 **SECTION 1. SHORT TITLE.**

2 This Act may be cited as the "Justice Against Spon-

3 sors of Terrorism Act".

4 **SEC. 2. FINDINGS AND PURPOSE.**

5 (a) FINDINGS.—Congress finds the following:

6 (1) International terrorism is a serious and

7 deadly problem that threatens the vital interests of

8 the United States.

9 (2) International terrorism affects the inter-

10 state and foreign commerce of the United States by

11 harming international trade and market stability,

12 and limiting international travel by United States

13 citizens as well as foreign visitors to the United

14 States.

15 (3) Some foreign terrorist organizations, acting

16 through affiliated groups or individuals, raise signifi-

17 cant funds outside of the United States for conduct

18 directed and targeted at the United States.

19 (4) It is necessary to recognize the substantive

20 causes of action for aiding and abetting and con-

21 spiracy liability under chapter 113B of title 18,

22 United States Code.

23 (5) The decision of the United States Court of

24 Appeals for the District of Columbia in Halberstam

25 v. Welch, 705 F.2d 472 (D.C. Cir. 1983), which has

26 been widely recognized as the leading case regarding

1 Federal civil aiding and abetting and conspiracy li-
2 ability, including by the Supreme Court of the
3 United States, provides the proper legal framework
4 for how such liability should function in the context
5 of chapter 113B of title 18, United States Code.

6 (6) Persons, entities, or countries that know-
7 ingly or recklessly contribute material support or re-
8 sources, directly or indirectly, to persons or organi-
9 zations that pose a significant risk of committing
10 acts of terrorism that threaten the security of na-
11 tionals of the United States or the national security,
12 foreign policy, or economy of the United States, nec-
13 essarily direct their conduct at the United States,
14 and should reasonably anticipate being brought to
15 court in the United States to answer for such activi-
16 ties.

17 (7) The United States has a vital interest in
18 providing persons and entities injured as a result of
19 terrorist attacks committed within the United States
20 with full access to the court system in order to pur-
21 sue civil claims against persons, entities, or countries
22 that have knowingly or recklessly provided material
23 support or resources, directly or indirectly, to the
24 persons or organizations responsible for their inju-
25 ries.

1   (b) PURPOSE.—The purpose of this Act is to provide

2 civil litigants with the broadest possible basis, consistent

3 with the Constitution of the United States, to seek relief

4 against persons, entities, and foreign countries, wherever

5 acting and wherever they may be found, that have pro-

6 vided material support, directly or indirectly, to foreign

7 organizations or persons that engage in terrorist activities

8 against the United States.

9 **SEC. 3. RESPONSIBILITY OF FOREIGN STATES FOR INTER-**

10 **NATIONAL TERRORISM AGAINST THE UNITED**

11 **STATES.**

12   (a) IN GENERAL.—Chapter 97 of title 28, United

13 States Code, is amended by inserting after section 1605A

14 the following:

15 **"§ 1605B. Responsibility of foreign states for inter-**

16 **national terrorism against the United**

17 **States**

18   "(a) DEFINITION.—In this section, the term 'inter-

19 national terrorism'—

20   "(1) has the meaning given the term in section

21   2331 of title 18, United States Code; and

22   "(2) does not include any act of war (as defined

23   in that section).

24   "(b) RESPONSIBILITY OF FOREIGN STATES.—A for-

25 eign state shall not be immune from the jurisdiction of

1 the courts of the United States in any case in which money
2 damages are sought against a foreign state for physical
3 injury to person or property or death occurring in the
4 United States and caused by—

5   "(1) an act of international terrorism in the
6   United States; and

7   "(2) a tortious act or acts of the foreign state,
8   or of any official, employee, or agent of that foreign
9   state while acting within the scope of his or her of-
10   fice, employment, or agency, regardless where the
11   tortious act or acts of the foreign state occurred.

12   "(c) CLAIMS BY NATIONALS OF THE UNITED
13 STATES.—Notwithstanding section 2337(2) of title 18, a
14 national of the United States may bring a claim against
15 a foreign state in accordance with section 2333 of that
16 title if the foreign state would not be immune under sub-
17 section (b).

18   "(d) RULE OF CONSTRUCTION.—A foreign state shall
19 not be subject to the jurisdiction of the courts of the
20 United States under subsection (b) on the basis of an
21 omission or a tortious act or acts that constitute mere neg-
22 ligence.".

23   (b) TECHNICAL AND CONFORMING AMENDMENTS.—
24   (1) The table of sections for chapter 97 of title
25   28, United States Code, is amended by inserting

1 after the item relating to section 1605A the fol-

2 lowing:

"1605B. Responsibility of foreign states for international terrorism against the United States.".

3   (2) Subsection 1605(g)(1)(A) of title 28,

4 United States Code, is amended by inserting "or

5 section 1605B" after "but for section 1605A".

6 **SEC. 4. AIDING AND ABETTING LIABILITY FOR CIVIL AC-**

7   **TIONS REGARDING TERRORIST ACTS.**

8   (a) IN GENERAL.—Section 2333 of title 18, United

9 States Code, is amended by adding at the end the fol-

10 lowing:

11   "(d) LIABILITY.—

12   "(1) DEFINITION.—In this subsection, the term

13   'person' has the meaning given the term in section

14   1 of title 1.

15   "(2) LIABILITY.—In an action under subsection

16   (a) for an injury arising from an act of international

17   terrorism committed, planned, or authorized by an

18   organization that had been designated as a foreign

19   terrorist organization under section 219 of the Im-

20   migration and Nationality Act (8 U.S.C. 1189), as

21   of the date on which such act of international ter-

22   rorism was committed, planned, or authorized, liabil-

23   ity may be asserted as to any person who aids and

24   abets, by knowingly providing substantial assistance,

1   or who conspires with the person who committed

2   such an act of international terrorism.".

3   (b) EFFECT ON FOREIGN SOVEREIGN IMMUNITIES

4 ACT.—Nothing in the amendment made by this section

5 affects immunity of a foreign state, as that term is defined

6 in section 1603 of title 28, United States Code, from juris-

7 diction under other law.

8 **SEC. 5. STAY OF ACTIONS PENDING STATE NEGOTIATIONS.**

9   (a) EXCLUSIVE JURISDICTION.—The courts of the

10 United States shall have exclusive jurisdiction in any ac-

11 tion in which a foreign state is subject to the jurisdiction

12 of a court of the United States under section 1605B of

13 title 28, United States Code, as added by section 3(a) of

14 this Act.

15   (b) INTERVENTION.—The Attorney General may in-

16 tervene in any action in which a foreign state is subject

17 to the jurisdiction of a court of the United States under

18 section 1605B of title 28, United States Code, as added

19 by section 3(a) of this Act, for the purpose of seeking a

20 stay of the civil action, in whole or in part.

21   (c) STAY.—

22   (1) IN GENERAL.—A court of the United States

23   may stay a proceeding against a foreign state if the

24   Secretary of State certifies that the United States is

25   engaged in good faith discussions with the foreign

1 state defendant concerning the resolution of the

2 claims against the foreign state, or any other parties

3 as to whom a stay of claims is sought.

4   (2) DURATION.—

5   (A) IN GENERAL.—A stay under this sec-

6   tion may be granted for not more than 180

7   days.

8   (B) EXTENSION.—

9   (i) IN GENERAL.—The Attorney Gen-

10   eral may petition the court for an exten-

11   sion of the stay for additional 180-day pe-

12   riods.

13   (ii) RECERTIFICATION.—A court shall

14   grant an extension under clause (i) if the

15   Secretary of State recertifies that the

16   United States remains engaged in good

17   faith discussions with the foreign state de-

18   fendant concerning the resolution of the

19   claims against the foreign state, or any

20   other parties as to whom a stay of claims

21   is sought.

22 **SEC. 6. SEVERABILITY.**

23   If any provision of this Act or any amendment made

24 by this Act, or the application of a provision or amend-

25 ment to any person or circumstance, is held to be invalid,

1 the remainder of this Act and the amendments made by

2 this Act, and the application of the provisions and amend-

3 ments to any other person not similarly situated or to

4 other circumstances, shall not be affected by the holding.

5 **SEC. 7. EFFECTIVE DATE.**

6 The amendments made by this Act shall apply to any

7 civil action—

8 (1) pending on, or commenced on or after, the

9 date of enactment of this Act; and

10 (2) arising out of an injury to a person, prop-

11 erty, or business on or after September 11, 2001.

Passed the Senate May 17, 2016.

Attest: JULIE E. ADAMS,

Secretary.

Mr. COHEN. Thank you, Mr. Chair. I welcome today's hearing on Senate Bill 2040, the "Justice Against Sponsors of Terrorism Act." The specific text was passed by the Senate, unanimous consent, May 17, 2016, but it did not receive a hearing or other formal vetting, so it is good that in the House we have a hearing, which is somewhat unusual for us.

S. 2040 would amend the Foreign Sovereign Immunities Act of 1976 to allow suits against foreign states for physical entry resulting from the act of international terrorism in the United States, and a tortious act on the part of the foreign state or its official employee or agent acting within the scope of his or her employment, wherever that act occurs.

The legislation also amends the Antiterrorism Act to explicitly provide for aiding and abetting liability. Finally, the bill contains a state provision allowing court to stay a case against a foreign state defender for up to 180 days; the possibility of an extension to go to a full year to allow the State Department to negotiate in good faith with the foreign state defendant to resolve the claims issued.

We have two panels of distinguished witnesses before us today, two folks from, I believe, both the diplomatic corps and the Mr. Mukasey, an outstanding former United States attorney, and then a buddy of Bob Brady's, which is almost equally in dignity to being a great former U.S. attorney.

And I hope that we can use this opportunity to learn about the bill to understand the detail of the arguments in its favor and the other potential conflicts. This is a difficult bill. You want to get justice for the victims of 9/11, but you also want to protect our national security.

The legislation arises from the litigation against various defendants concerning 9/11. Legislation is drafted in general terms. We consider it in that light as both the supporters and opponents seem to agree.

I am for access to justice and always have been, and it is my inclination to support such measures, and it is also my inclination to support, in any way I can, the victims of the dastardly deeds of 9/11. And it is particularly strong in that case, because that is something that we all experienced and should not get out of our psyches and our minds.

The bill supporters argue that it is needed to update laws to address cases where foreign states facilitate terrorist strikes in the United States through financing and other kinds of material support for foreign terrorist organizations like Al-Qaeda. They also assert the bill would deter such conduct in the future, thereby enhancing counterterrorism efforts.

They further contend that the Senate-passed language is narrow in scope, and the concerns about any reciprocal effects from enacting this legislation are exaggerated. The Obama administration, however, continues to raise concerns, even in the admitted form that we consider today, and I take that seriously as well.

In addition to the reciprocity concern, the Administration contends enactment of Senate Bill 2040 could undermine counterterrorism efforts, raise serious foreign policy concerns, and lead to a reduction of foreign investment in the United States.

Some opponents further argue that enacting this bill could subject U.S. allies to liability in the U.S. courts, including countries like Britain and Israel.

Both sides have come forth with seemingly strong arguments, and while I appreciate the fact the Senate passed this language by voice vote, I think it is worth our while to have a discussion about the merits of S. 2040, and I thank the Chairman for having that hearing. I thank our witnesses for being here. I am looking forward to the testimony.

Mr. FRANKS. And I thank the gentleman, and I would now yield to the Chairman of the Committee, Mr. Goodlatte, from Virginia.

Mr. GOODLATTE. Well, thank you, Mr. Chairman, and I want to begin by thanking Ambassador Patterson and Mr. Egan for appearing before the Committee today on behalf of the State Department. I know that the department has some foreign policy-related concerns with this legislation, and we wanted through this hearing to give the department the opportunity to express those concerns.

The Justice Against Sponsors of Terrorism Act has been introduced over several successive congresses, and has twice unanimously passed the Senate. Over the years that this legislation has been considered, we have worked with its sponsors and the Senate Judiciary Committee to make the bill's language more precise in order to ensure that any unintended consequences are kept to a minimum.

In particular, I have worked to make sure that JASTA's extension of secondary liability under the Antiterrorism Act closely tracks the common-law standard for aiding and abetting liability and is limited to State Department-designated foreign terrorist organizations.

Aiding and abetting liability should only attach under the ATA to persons who have actual knowledge that they are directly providing substantial assistance to a designated foreign terrorist organization, in connection with the organization's commission of an act of international terrorism. JASTA, as revised in the Senate Judiciary Committee, ensures that aiding and abetting liability is limited in this manner.

Beyond the Antiterrorism Act, JASTA amends the Foreign Sovereign Immunities Act in order to waive the sovereign immunity of any foreign government that sponsors an act of international terrorism that both causes physical injury in the United States, and occurs on U.S. soil.

JASTA makes this change because under current law, a foreign Nation can provide financing and other substantial assistance to a terrorist organization that attacks our country and escape liability so long as all of the material support is provided overseas.

For example, under current law, if a foreign state or any official or employee of that foreign state sets off a bomb on U.S. soil, injuring our citizens, the country would be liable under the Foreign Sovereign Immunities Act's tort exception. However, if we change the fact pattern slightly, so that rather than directly setting of the bomb, the foreign state instead gives a foreign terrorist organization the money it needs to attack the United States, the foreign state will not be subject to liability in U.S. courts.

This is a troubling loophole in our antiterrorism laws. When Congress enacted the Foreign Sovereign Immunities Act in 1976, it put in place a broad set of exceptions to sovereign immunity, including an exception for tort claims involving injuries occurring in the United States.

However, the courts have not consistently interpreted those exceptions in such a manner that they cover the sponsoring of a terrorist attack on U.S. soil. JASTA attempts to address this inconsistency with a concrete rule.

I am interested to hear, however, from the State Department as to why JASTA's amendments to the Foreign Sovereign Immunities Act present a threat to our relationships with countries that are important partners in combatting terrorism.

Certainly, we do not want to make it more difficult for the State Department, the Department of Defense, and other agencies to combat global terrorism, but at the same time, we do not want to have laws in place that make it impossible for U.S. citizens who are victims of terrorist attacks on U.S. soil to seek judicial redress against those who seek to harm us. I look forward to our witnesses' testimony on this important subject, and yield back the balance of my time.

Mr. FRANKS. And I thank the gentleman, and I would now yield to the Ranking Member of the Committee, Mr. Conyers from Michigan.

Mr. CONYERS. Thank, Mr. Chairman. Members of the Committee, without question, the victims of the September 11 terrorist attack deserve our sympathy and our help, and this Committee has worked to enact interlaw measures that attempt to provide some relief to these victims. As we consider S. 2040, the Justice Against Sponsors of Terrorism Act, we must keep in mind that this legislation is written in general terms, and we should consider its impact beyond one case, however compelling that case may be.

Among other things, S. 2040 amends the Foreign Sovereign Immunities Act to create a new exception to the Act's general grant of foreign sovereign immunity. The exception would apply to claims arising from physical injury as a result of an act of international terrorism in the United States, as well as to a tortious act of a foreign state or its official, employee, or agent acting within his or her official capacity, regardless of where the tortious act took place.

The House has not previously held a hearing on this proposal, and neither chamber has held a hearing on this particular version of the legislation, so I approach this measure with an open mind. That being said, there are three overarching points that should inform our discussion today.

To begin with, the purpose of sovereign immunity is to ensure that disputes among Nations are ultimately resolved through diplomatic efforts rather than litigation. Customary international law provided absolute immunity for states in the courts of other states.

Nevertheless, in the last century, many countries, including the United States, came to realize that it was unfair to provide immunity in cases where countries were engaged in non-sovereign activities, such as ordinary commerce.

For this reason, countries began recognizing certain limited exceptions to sovereign immunity. The Foreign Sovereign Immunities

Act codified the customary law of sovereign immunity recognized by our country at the time of the Act's enactment in 1976, including certain exceptions to sovereign immunity.

The Act also removed the need for, and the ability of the State Department, to make case-by-case determinations of whether a foreign state defendant was entitled to sovereign immunity and left such determination to courts as a matter of statutory interpretation, which in theory depoliticized such determinations.

In light of this history, we should consider what impact changing the scope of exceptions to sovereign immunity may have on United States interests. The Administration, some allied Nations, and others have raised the concern that the enactment of S. 2040 may lead to retaliation by other countries against the United States, given the breadth of our interests and expansive reach of our global activities.

For example, they contend a country like Afghanistan or Pakistan, under a future hostile regime, may enact legislation abrogating sovereign immunity to allow suits against the United States, against United States officials, or even our military personnel in response to drone strikes, or other activities in their countries.

The bill's supporters, on the other hand, argue that the already-existing exceptions to sovereign immunity, including the current state-sponsored terrorism exception, and the prior understanding of the tort exception, that this bill purports to restore, have not resulted in any meaningful retaliation against the United States.

So, finally, we should consider the impact this measure may have on our Nation's counterterrorism efforts. The bill's proponents argue that it will enhance such efforts by raising the prospect of depriving terrorists of resources, and deterring future terrorism financing.

On the other hand, others say that it will hamper cooperation from other countries because they may become more reluctant to share sensitive intelligence in light of the greater risks that such information may be revealed in litigation.

While this bill and the underlying litigation that spawned it arose from an emotionally searing event, I hope that we can be both respectful and clear-eyed as we consider the arguments to be presented by our distinguished witnesses. And so accordingly, I look forward to an engaging debate, and I thank our witnesses for being with us to share their thoughts on these important issues. I thank the Chair.

Mr. FRANKS. And I thank the gentleman, and without objection, other Members' opening statements will be made a part of the record.

So, let me now introduce our witnesses. We have two very distinguished panels today. I will begin by the first panel.

Our first witness is Ambassador Anne Patterson, the Assistant Secretary of State for Near East Affairs. Ambassador Patterson has served as the U.S. ambassador to four countries, and in 2008 was promoted to the rank of career ambassador, the highest rank in foreign service. She has served as Assistant Secretary of State for International Narcotics and Law Enforcement Affairs, and has served as Deputy Permanent Representative at the U.S. mission to the United Nations.

Our second witness is Brian Egan, the legal adviser to the State Department. Prior to being appointed as legal adviser, Mr. Egan served as legal adviser to the National Security Council, Deputy Assistant to the President, and Deputy Counsel to the President, and as Assistant General Counsel for Enforcement Intelligence at the Department of the Treasury.

Each of the witnesses' written statements will be entered into the record in its entirety, and I would ask that each witness summarize his or her testimony in 5 minutes or less. To help you stay within the time, there is a timing light in front of you. The light will switch from green to yellow, indicating that you have 1 minute to conclude your testimony. When the light turns red, it indicates that the witness' 5 minutes have expired.

So, before I recognize the witnesses, it is the tradition of the Subcommittee that they be sworn. So, if you would please stand and be sworn.

Do you solemnly swear that the testimony that you are about to give will be the truth, the whole truth, and nothing but the truth, so help you God? You may be seated.

Let the record reflect that the witnesses answered in the affirmative, and I welcome both of you. And I now recognize our first witness, Ambassador Patterson; and Ambassador, if you might turn that microphone on before speaking.

TESTIMONY OF ANNE W. PATTERSON, ASSISTANT SECRETARY OF STATE FOR NEAR EASTERN AFFAIRS, U.S. DEPARTMENT OF STATE

Ms. PATTERSON. Okay, thank you, Chairman Franks, Ranking Member Cohen, Members of the Subcommittee. Thank you for inviting us to appear before you today to discuss the Justice Against Sponsors of Terrorism Act. I welcome the opportunity to testify with my colleague, Brian Egan, the Department of State's legal adviser.

I understand the motivation for this legislation, and all of us in the Administration deeply sympathize with the victims of terror and their families. I can personally attest that unprecedented resources have been dedicated to our national security to ensure that no other Americans will suffer the same fate as the victims of the September 11th attacks.

From the successful efforts against Al-Qaeda leadership in the Pakistan-Afghanistan border, to the vast improvement in our intelligence about terrorist leaders, and to our successes in rooting out sources of funding for terrorism, we have worked every day to protect the homeland. We all know that the families of the 9/11 victims have suffered grievously, and nothing will ever be sufficient to alleviate their suffering. However, the 9/11 attacks were, and have continued to be the subject of intense and exhaustive investigation by U.S. government agencies and commissions.

While these efforts will continue, I am here today to explain why the Administration believes that JASTA is not the right path forward. Most importantly, the passage of JASTA could undermine our critical fight against terrorism, and particularly against ISIL, by limiting our flexibility in operating overseas, and thereby threaten our national security interests.

JASTA represents a sea change in longstanding principles, and would allow private litigations against foreign governments in U.S. courts, based on allegations that such countries' actions abroad made them responsible for terrorism-related injuries on U.S. soil. This legislation would allow suits against countries that have neither been designated by the executive branch as state sponsors of terrorism, nor taken direct action in the United States to carry out an attack here.

JASTA would hinder our ability to protect our national security interests by damaging relationships with countries that are important, critical partners in combatting terrorism at a crucial time when we are trying to build coalitions, not create divisions. We cannot win the fight against ISIL without full international cooperation to deny ISIL safe haven, disrupt its finances, counter its violent messaging, and share intelligence on its activities.

Numerous European and Middle Eastern governments have reached out to the department to express their concerns about this bill. The Dutch Parliament unanimously passed a motion on July 6th calling JASTA a breach of Dutch sovereignty that could expose the Netherlands to astronomically high damages via exposure to liability in U.S. courts.

I have seen firsthand throughout my career that the United States benefits significantly from the protection afforded by foreign sovereign immunity given its extensive diplomatic security and assistance operations.

We believe, just as importantly, that this legislation opens the U.S. to litigation abroad. As Members of this Committee know, some actions the United States takes overseas can be controversial, and if JASTA is enacted, it could erode our sovereign immunity protections abroad. Even if they are not eager to do so—and in many cases foreign governments are fully supportive of the counterterrorism steps the United States has taken—such governments will come under intense public pressure to create rights for their citizens to soothe the United States.

As you know, the United States funds, trains, and equips numerous groups around the world. Exposing the United States to lawsuits in foreign courts could open the door to litigation seeking claims against the U.S. government and reduce our ability to work with groups that have been vital to achieving our national security objectives.

U.S. counterterrorism strikes that have been a crucial and successful component of our counter-Al-Qaeda and counter-ISIL efforts do occasionally, tragically, and despite all safeguards, cause civilian casualties. If foreign courts were to take a similar approach in a country where such a strike took place, they might allow suits to be brought against the United States for such actions.

Additionally, men and women working on such operations could face the risk of being brought to trial or compelled to provide evidence if they travel to the country where the operation occurred. We have deep concerns about exposing this broad range of U.S. national security-related conduct to scrutiny in foreign courts. These risks could ultimately have a chilling effect on our own counterterrorism efforts.

Finally, I want to mention the possibility that JASTA may cause foreign governments to reconsider their investments here because they may have concerns that their money would be at risk of being attached in connection with a lawsuit. Before proceeding with this legislation, we believe there needs to be additional consideration of the potential unintended consequences of its enactment.

We welcome opportunities to engage with the Subcommittee on that discussion. I also want to thank the Subcommittee for your ongoing support as we continue to advance our national security interests, and I look forward to answering your questions.

[The prepared statement of Ms. Patterson follows:]

Statement for the Record
Ambassador Anne W. Patterson
Assistant Secretary of State for Near Eastern Affairs

House Judiciary Committee
Subcommittee on the Constitution and Civil Justice
July 14, 2016

Chairman Franks, Ranking Member Cohen, Members of the Subcommittee, thank you for inviting us to appear before you today to discuss the Justice Against Sponsors of Terrorism Act. I welcome the opportunity to testify with my colleague, Brian Egan, the Department of State's Legal Advisor.

I understand the motivation for the Justice Against Sponsors of Terrorism Act, and all of us in the Administration deeply sympathize with victims of terror and with their families. The State Department has long supported efforts to obtain compensation for U.S. terrorism victims, while also leading international efforts to combat terrorism and prevent more attacks against the homeland and our citizens abroad. I can personally attest that enormous focus and resources have been dedicated to addressing this threat so no other Americans will suffer the same fate as the victims of the September 11th attacks. From the successful efforts against Al Qaeda leadership in the Pakistan-Afghanistan border area, to the vast improvement in our intelligence about terrorist leaders; to the increasingly close and mutually beneficial cooperation with allies; and to our successes in rooting out sources of funding for terrorists, we have worked every day to protect America.

We know that the families of the 9/11 victims have suffered grievously. From the establishment of the original U.S. government compensation fund to today, we have been resolute in uniting to protect our country and to bring to justice those responsible for the attacks. The 9/11 attacks were, and have continued to be, the subject of intense and exhaustive investigation by U.S. government agencies and commissions.

While all of these efforts will continue, I am here today to explain the Administration's strong conviction that JASTA is not the right path forward. Most importantly, the passage of JASTA could undermine our critical fight against terrorism and particularly against ISIL by limiting our flexibility in operating overseas. It could potentially expose the U.S. government to billions of dollars in claims; it raises serious foreign policy concerns; and it could lead to a slowdown of foreign investments in the United States.

The current version of JASTA represents a sea change in longstanding principles which could have serious implications for U.S. interests. JASTA would allow private litigation against foreign governments in U.S. courts based on allegations that such countries' actions *abroad* made them responsible for terrorism-related injuries on U.S soil. This legislation would allow suits against countries that have neither been designated by the Executive Branch as state sponsors of terrorism nor taken direct actions in the United States to carry out an attack here. JASTA would hinder our ability to protect our national security interests by damaging relationships with countries that are important partners in combating terrorism, at a crucial time when we are trying to build coalitions, not create divisions. We cannot win the fight against ISIL without full international cooperation to deny ISIL safe haven, disrupt its finances, counter its violent messaging, and share intelligence on its activities. Our close and effective cooperation with other countries, both bilaterally and through multilateral vehicles such as the 66-member Global Coalition to Counter-ISIL, could be seriously hindered.

With the broad reach of JASTA, there is the likelihood that some of our critical allies, such as the United Kingdom or other European governments, could face lawsuits in U.S. courts which could affect their cooperation with us, as well as their broader bilateral relationship with us.

Numerous European and Middle Eastern governments have reached out to the Department to express their concerns about the bill. The parliament in the Netherlands unanimously passed a motion on July 6 calling JASTA a "breach of Dutch sovereignty" that could expose the Netherlands to "astronomically high damages" via exposure to liability in U.S. courts and called on the government to potentially convey its concerns about JASTA to the United States. A British Member of Parliament, Thomas Tugendhat, in an opinion piece last month in the UK's *Telegraph* newspaper, wrote that the bill "could also have serious unintended consequences for Britain. The act would expose the British government to the possibility of revealing the secrets of intelligence operations in open court, or paying damages over alleged failures to prevent terrorist attacks. Either outcome would put the special relationship under severe strain." He expressed the view that it might be used by U.S. citizens to bring suit against the British government for failure "to tackle Islamic radicalism in earlier decades" by not addressing the problem of radical Islamic preachers in the UK, which he notes some say spawned terrorism.

The bill also poses a serious threat to U.S. interests overseas. I have seen firsthand throughout my career at my postings around the world that the United States benefits significantly from the protection afforded by foreign sovereign immunity given its extensive diplomatic, security, and assistance operations. As members of this committee know from their extensive travels abroad, some actions the United States takes overseas are controversial with local citizens and foreign governments. If JASTA is enacted, it could erode our sovereign immunity protections abroad, as some foreign governments will rush to pass similar legislation to allow claims against the United States and its property, and in some cases, even against U.S. officials. Even if they are not eager to do so – in many cases foreign governments are fully supportive of steps the United States has taken –such governments will come under intense public pressure to create rights for their citizens to sue the United States. As the world's largest economy, the United States has extensive operations overseas, including property ownership, and thus is particularly vulnerable to asset seizures abroad.

The United States funds, trains, or equips numerous counter-terrorism, military, intelligence and law enforcement groups around the world. These groups are essential partners for the United States. As I saw first-hand when I served as Ambassador to Pakistan and Colombia such groups have been courageous in confronting terrorists in Pakistan and in uncovering terrorists and combatting narco-traffickers in Colombia. Likewise they are bravely fighting ISIL in Iraq right now. Exposing the United States to lawsuits in foreign courts with regard to the actions of such groups could open the door to intrusive litigation seeking billions of dollars of claims against the U.S. government and could reduce our ability to work with groups that have been vital to achieving our national security goals. U.S. counterterrorism strikes that have been a crucial and successful component of our counter- Al Qaeda and counter-ISIL efforts do occasionally, tragically and despite all our safeguards, cause civilian casualties. If foreign courts were to take a JASTA-like approach in the country where such a strike took place, they might allow suits to be brought against the United States for such actions. Additionally, men and women working on such operations could face the risk of being brought to trial or compelled to provide evidence if they traveled to the country where the operation occurred.

We have deep concerns about exposing this broad range of U.S. national security-related conduct to scrutiny in foreign courts. These risks could ultimately have a chilling effect on our own counter-terrorism efforts.

In the course of my 42-year career, I have encountered a number of situations in which legislation like JASTA could have interfered with important U.S. government efforts overseas. Notwithstanding the care that we take in designing our training programs, I have seen abuses committed by rogue elements of groups we have trained which resulted in civilian casualties; I have worked with courageous Americans and others associated with the U.S. government who were involved in dangerous and risky operations. The U.S. military supports allied efforts which at times have regretfully resulted in civilian casualties, which some may allege were wrongful. Perhaps more common than actual abuses, I have heard frequent claims that the U.S. government "should have known" about some abuse that took place, given its allegedly close relationship with elements of the local government or the alleged reach of its intelligence operation. If the principle of sovereign immunity is eroded, foreign courts could enter into an extensive range of suits and discovery against the United States, putting U.S. personnel and property in a precarious situation.

Finally, I want to mention the possibility that JASTA may cause foreign governments to hesitate to invest or maintain their funds in the United States. The administration actively encourages foreign investment in the United States, as high-profile events like Select USA demonstrate. We have the world's largest and most open economy and take pride in the preeminence of New York as a financial center. Opening up U.S. courts to JASTA-type cases may cause foreign states to think twice about their investments here because they may have concerns that their money would be at risk of being attached in connection with a lawsuit. Foreign governments may simply decide to avoid this risk by keeping their assets outside of the U.S. financial system or avoiding dollar denominated transactions. This is what happened in in 2007 when Iraq threatened to remove its assets from the United States in response to a provision in the NDAA that would have exposed Iraq to potential liability. That prompted a Presidential veto and a later Congressional response adding a waiver for Iraq.

In sum, JASTA could have a serious negative impact on U.S. efforts to fight terrorism and could expose our allies and partners to lawsuits in U.S. courts, which could reduce their willingness to cooperate with us on crucial issues of U.S. national security. I am fully sympathetic to the desire of victims of terrorism to gain justice for their loved ones. However, this bill is not the solution. Before proceeding with the legislation, we believe there needs to be additional, careful consideration of the potential unintended consequences of its enactment. We welcome opportunities to engage with this Subcommittee on that discussion. I also want to thank this Subcommittee for your ongoing support as we continue to advance our national security interests and I look forward to answering your questions.

———————

Mr. FRANKS. And I thank the gentlelady, and I will now recognize our second witness, Mr. Egan. Sir, if you will turn that microphone on before speaking, as well.

TESTIMONY OF THE HONORABLE BRIAN EGAN, LEGAL ADVISER, U.S. DEPARTMENT OF STATE

Mr. EGAN. Thank you, Chairman Franks, Ranking Member Cohen, and Members of the Subcommittee. I also appreciate the opportunity to appear before you with my colleague, Assistant Secretary Anne Patterson, to discuss the Justice Against Sponsors of Terrorism Act.

At the outset, I would like to express my deep sympathy for the families whose loved ones perished in the attacks on September 11th. I grew up in a community in New Jersey that was deeply affected by the World Trade Center attacks, and for much of my career in government at the Departments of State and Treasury, and at the National Security Council, I have worked on mechanisms that would enable our government to confront terrorism, including financial sanctions, and the use of military force where appropriate.

I am going to focus my comments today on the importance of the concept of sovereign immunity to the United States, and our concern that passage of JASTA will lead to harmful, reciprocal—excuse me—legislation and lawsuits against the United States overseas.

The principle of sovereign immunity, which restricts lawsuits against foreign governments, is well-accepted in international law, and was long recognized by U.S. courts as a matter of common law. The United States benefits greatly from the protection afforded by foreign sovereign immunity, and the Department of Justice regularly and vigorously defends our sovereign immunity overseas.

Over the years, Congress and the executive branch have worked together to approach issues of foreign sovereign immunity and exceptions with great caution. The Foreign Sovereign Immunities Act, or FSIA, was enacted in 1976, following many years of study and consultation between Congress and the executive branch, academics, the American Bar Association, and private practitioners.

The act focuses on the narrow instances in which a foreign state's immunity is denied. For example, a foreign state's commercial activities in the United States or having direct effects here.

The narrow, noncommercial tort exception to immunity was aimed primarily at the problem of traffic accidents, and it provides jurisdiction for torts committed by foreign governments inside the United States that result in injuries here.

Later enacted provisions relating to terrorism prudentially restrict the ability to sue foreign governments in U.S. courts for acts undertaken abroad to those states that have been designated by the executive branch as state sponsors of terrorism: currently Iran, Sudan, and Syria.

JASTA would represent a significant departure from this carefully crafted framework. JASTA would strip any foreign government of its sovereign immunity, and expose the relevant country to lawsuits in U.S. courts based on allegations in the lawsuit that the country's actions abroad made it responsible for an attack on U.S.

soil. As Ambassador Patterson noted, a number of U.S. partners and allies have raised concerns about the potential consequences of this change.

The adoption of legislation like JASTA likely would have reciprocal consequences for the United States and increase our country's vulnerability to lawsuits overseas. Reciprocity plays a substantial role in foreign relations. JASTA could encourage foreign courts to exercise jurisdiction over the United States or U.S. officials for allegedly causing injuries overseas through groups we support as part of our counterterrorism efforts, circumstances in which we properly would consider ourselves to be immune.

Notwithstanding the care with which the United States operates to ensure that its actions overseas are appropriately calibrated, exposing U.S. national security-related conduct and decision-making to scrutiny in foreign courts would present significant concerns. Such litigation would have the potential for intrusive requests for sensitive U.S. documents and witnesses that we would not be willing to provide. There is a risk of sizeable monetary damages awards in such cases, which could then lead to efforts to attach U.S. government property in far-flung places.

Given the broad range of U.S. activities and presence around the world, the United States is a much larger target for such litigation than any other country. We stand ready to work with this Subcommittee and other Members of Congress to consider these important issues further, and I look forward to taking your questions. Thank you.

[The prepared statement of Mr. Egan follows:]

Statement for the Record
Department of State
Legal Adviser Brian Egan

House Judiciary Committee
Subcommittee on the Constitution and Civil Justice
July 14, 2016

Thank you, Chairman Franks, Ranking Member Cohen, and Members of the
Subcommittee. I appreciate the opportunity to appear before you with my
colleague, Assistant Secretary Anne Patterson, to discuss the views of the
Department of State on the Justice Against Sponsors of Terrorism Act.

At the outset, I would like to express my deep sympathy for the families whose
loved ones perished in the attacks on September 11. I grew up in a bedroom
community in New Jersey that was deeply affected by the World Trade Center
attacks. For much of my career in government, at the Departments of State and
Treasury and the National Security Council, I have worked on mechanisms that
enable our government to confront terrorism, including financial sanctions and the
use of military force where appropriate.

I will focus my comments today on the importance of the concept of sovereign
immunity to the United States, and our concern that passage of JASTA will lead to
harmful, reciprocal legislation and lawsuits against the United States overseas.

The principle of sovereign immunity, which restricts lawsuits against foreign
governments, is well accepted in international law and was long recognized by
U.S. courts as a matter of common law. The United States benefits greatly from
the protection afforded by foreign sovereign immunity, and the Department of
Justice regularly and vigorously defends our sovereign immunity overseas. Over
the years, Congress and the Executive Branch have worked together to approach
issues of foreign sovereign immunity and its exceptions with great caution.

The Foreign Sovereign Immunities Act, or FSIA, was enacted in 1976 following
many years of study and consultation between Congress and the Executive Branch,
academics, the American Bar Association, and private practitioners. The Act
focuses on the narrow instances in which a foreign state's immunity is denied: for
example, a foreign state's commercial activities in the United States or having
direct effects here. The narrow non-commercial tort exception to immunity was
aimed primarily at the problem of traffic accidents, and it provides jurisdiction for

torts committed by foreign governments *inside* the United States that result in injuries here. Later enacted provisions relating to terrorism prudently restrict the ability to sue foreign governments in U.S. courts for acts undertaken abroad to those States that have been designated by the Executive branch as state sponsors of terrorism – currently Iran, Sudan, and Syria.

JASTA would represent a significant departure from this carefully crafted framework. JASTA would strip any foreign government of its sovereign immunity and expose the relevant country to lawsuits in U.S. courts based on allegations in the lawsuit that the country's actions *abroad* made it responsible for an attack on U.S soil. As Ambassador Patterson noted, a number of U.S. partners and allies have raised concerns about the potential consequences of this change.

The adoption of legislation like JASTA likely would have reciprocal consequences for the United States and increase our country's vulnerability to lawsuits overseas. Reciprocity plays a substantial role in foreign relations. JASTA could encourage foreign courts to exercise jurisdiction over the United States or U.S. officials for allegedly causing injuries overseas through groups we support as part of our counter-terrorism efforts – circumstances in which we properly would consider ourselves to be immune.

Notwithstanding the care with which the United States operates to ensure that its actions overseas are appropriately calibrated, exposing U.S. national security-related conduct and decision-making to scrutiny in foreign courts would present significant concerns. Such litigation would have the potential for intrusive requests for sensitive U.S. documents and witnesses that we would not be willing to provide. There is a risk of sizeable monetary damages awards in such cases, which could then lead to efforts to attach U.S. government property in far-flung places. Given the broad range of U.S. activities and presence around the world, the United States is a much larger target for such litigation than any other country.

We stand ready to work with this subcommittee and other members of Congress to consider these important issues further. I look forward to taking your questions.

Mr. FRANKS. Well, I thank you both for your testimony. We will now proceed under the 5 minute rule with questions, and I will begin by recognizing myself for 5 minutes.

Ambassador, I will begin with you. In my opening statement, I mentioned several of the nine exceptions to foreign sovereign immunity that are provided for in the Foreign Sovereign Immunities Act, including the exception for lawsuits against a foreign state for personal injury or death occurring in the United States. From a foreign policy perspective, what is the difference between the already existing exceptions, especially the tort exception, and the new exceptions proposed by JASTA?

And Mr. Egan, if you will prepare, I would like to ask you the same question afterwards. Ambassador? You are going to defer to him? All right.

Mr. EGAN. Mr. Chairman, thanks for that question. I think that the primary difference between the existing exception that you referenced and the change that JASTA would make would be twofold. One would be under the tort exception now. The activity that caused the tort in the United States would have to take place within the United States itself.

And as I mentioned in my testimony, I think this exception was originally created by Congress to address torts that occur, such as traffic accidents, here in the United States.

The change here would be subjecting decisions that may take place overseas and actions overseas in a way that they are not currently covered by current law, and that is the nature—the focus of our concern is on that change.

Mr. FRANKS. Well, let me just follow up on that. I would like to ask you a question that was posed to me by the family of a victim of the September 11th terrorist attack. And essentially if a foreign state, such as Saudi Arabia, knowingly plays a substantial role in a terrorist attack on U.S. soil, do the victims of such an attack not deserve to be able to bring a lawsuit against that foreign state in U.S. courts?

I mean, why would the victims of a terrorist attack on U.S. soil be given less access to justice for their claims than is granted, for example—under the example that you used, sir, to the victims of a car wreck caused by a foreign government, for which the foreign state may be held accountable under the FSIA's tort exception?

Mr. EGAN. Mr. Chairman, first of all, I do not pretend to stand in the shoes of the 9/11 families, and I understand the need to do everything we can for those families. I think our concern is really the breadth that this expansion of the exception could cause. By subjecting decision making and other operations overseas to our courts, we would be inviting other countries to do the same. We know that other countries follow what we do under the FSIA and with respect to sovereign immunity with great interest, and our concern is that that sort of change could lead to reciprocal actions that would affect our own operations and decision making.

Mr. FRANKS. Reciprocal actions are your primary fear?

Mr. EGAN. I will let Ambassador Patterson speak to the foreign policy and national security concerns we have from our partners. And I am happy to say more about the reciprocal concerns that we have.

Ms. PATTERSON. Mr. Chairman, in the case of Saudi Arabia, let me say that neither the 9/11 Commission nor the review that was undertaken of the 9/11 Commission in 2015 found any link between the 9/11 attack and the government of Saudi Arabia.

But if such a link should, of course, arise at any point—and again I stress that there is absolutely no evidence there was such a link—the U.S. government would pursue that vigorously through all kinds of methods—law enforcement, intelligence, seizure of assets. I believe there is sort of the undercurrent here that we do not have tools existing to go after these cases.

And over the past 15 years, we have employed a very broad range and aggressive range of tools to go after these 9/11 perpetrators and to change the international system that allows terrorist financing to prosper. So, I think the presumption is mistaken, but I also think if that were proven to be true, we would do everything in our power to seek redress.

Mr. FRANKS. And do you have any examples of going after a sovereign Nation that supported terrorism on a civil action in the U.S. courts?

Mr. EGAN. So, Mr. Chairman, as you know, under the existing terrorism exception, cases are allowed against countries that are designated as state sponsors of terrorism, and that exception has been used. Our view is that that is a prudential approach to this very difficult program.

Mr. FRANKS. Let me just expand on that. Why would the law treat such an act of terrorism that kills people on U.S. soil differently depending on whether the substantial assistance was provided by a designated state sponsor of terrorism or a Nation that is not so designated?

Mr. EGAN. The existing exception was crafted between Congress and the executive branch to allow for a decision and evidence to be looked at by the executive branch as to whether the relevant government has repeatedly provided support for acts of international terrorism. We think that is an important check on the process, and it is one that would change with this law.

Mr. FRANKS. All right, I now recognize the Ranking Member for his 5 minutes for questioning.

Mr. COHEN. Thank you. Mr. Egan, Saudi Arabia is not on the list, right?

Mr. EGAN. That is correct, sir.

Mr. COHEN. And if change this law, and they are subject to liability, might we find out that they should have been on the list? I mean, it is just asking a question, you know. And my colleagues on the Republican side, they had some law this year that said that if you have gone to certain countries and you come here, you cannot do it unless you go through all this kind of security checks because it is such a danger, and they did not put Saudi Arabia on that list either.

Ms. PATTERSON. Mr.——

Mr. COHEN. Sure, anybody can answer it.

Ms. PATTERSON. Mr. Cohen, again, I would stress that there is absolutely no evidence that the Saudis have been involved in the 9/11 attacks, and we have a very close——

Mr. COHEN. But if they are not, are they not going to win the lawsuit?

Ms. PATTERSON. The lawsuit——

Mr. COHEN. Ms. Patterson, go ahead.

Ms. PATTERSON. So, I think our concerns about this legislation are broad, and that this is—first of all, Saudi Arabia and many other countries in the Middle East are very important partners in our fight against terrorism——

Mr. COHEN. I am going to interrupt you for a second because they are as threatened, if not more threatened, by ISIL as we are. They are right there with them. They have been knocking off Saudis, and they have got no love for them either. Are you submitting that if we pass this that the Saudis are going to stop fighting ISIL and stop working with us? I think they have got an interest in fighting ISIL, too, do they not?

Ms. PATTERSON. Absolutely.

Mr. COHEN. So if they absolutely had this right, but they are going to—it is going to harm our abilities to fight ISIL, then it is just not such a good partner we got.

Ms. PATTERSON. Mr. Cohen, the Saudis, over the past 15 years, have instituted a very broad range of steps that have cut off financing for terrorists, and I could outline those here. They have cooperated with us very extensively on intelligence exchanges and intelligence tips that have protected American citizens, and again, they are on the forefront of this fight against terrorism, as you mentioned. They are a very important partner in our fight against terrorism.

Mr. COHEN. What leads you to believe that they would not be? It's in their self-interest to be. They do everything for their self-interest, including selling us oil, which we have been slaves to, and that is why they are not on the list.

Ms. PATTERSON. Sir, I would take issue with that. They are not on the list, because they are not a state sponsor of terrorism, and the process of designating state sponsors of terrorism is an exhaustive and analytical one. There is a very significant difference between Saudi Arabia and the countries that are on the list of state sponsors of terrorism.

Mr. COHEN. Okay, I agree with you on that. Cuba is on the list, did they not?

Ms. PATTERSON. No longer.

Mr. COHEN. They just came off, right? And they were a real threat to us. Great list. And I understand the difference, but at the same time we did pass this bill on the folks that wanted to come here to visit, and the Saudis were not on it, and the only folks that we know that we came here from a foreign country that did us some damage, who we should have kept out, were from there. And you may totally be right, and I do not know.

I am not going to comment on the 28 pages, and that might influence people pro, con, I do not know what. Who knows? But the lawsuit is only going to bring that information, and it is real limited, is it not?

Ms. PATTERSON. Sir, I think the 28 pages will be very shortly released, and Members of this Committee and members of the public can judge for themselves. But it is not just Saudis who have come to this state to commit terrorist attacks.

When I was ambassador to Pakistan, we had two very dramatic events. One, the so-called Times Square bomber, who was a Pakistani, and an Afghan in Colorado who was going to bomb the New York subway station. And in both cases, the cooperation of foreign intelligence agencies was absolutely vital in running down and analyzing and preventing these attacks. So, yes, we have certainly the terrorist threat, but it is much broader than Saudi Arabia.

Mr. COHEN. Let me ask you one other question. You talked about litigation abroad that we could be subject to. Basically, is that State Department talk for drones?

Ms. PATTERSON. It is not just drones, sir.

Mr. COHEN. What else do we do that we could be sued?

Ms. PATTERSON. Okay, then let me outline, then, if I could. It is drones. Certainly, it is drones. It is some of these organizations, these law enforcement and intelligence and military organizations that we support, but it is also the fact—when I was in Egypt in 2011, International Republican Institute and National Democratic Institute were prosecuted in Egyptian courts on criminal charges.

It is also because we do not trust, in many cases, the legal systems and the prosecutors and the kangaroo courts in these other countries, and we could easily have a lawsuit brought about by corrupt or intimidated judges or by the public that could prejudice U.S. interests. It is not just people that get killed. It is a whole range of other activities that we engage in.

Mr. COHEN. My time has expired, and I yield back the balance of it.

Mr. FRANKS. And I thank the gentleman. It is interesting to note that only after we had moved to normalize relations with Cuba did we take them off the terrorist list. I now recognize the Ranking Member of the Committee, Mr. Conyers, for 5 minutes.

Mr. CONYERS. Thank you, Mr. Chairman, and I thank the witnesses. Let me begin with the ambassador and the—I wanted to ask about—Egan first—all right, I will start with Mr. Egan first. Sir, the bill's supporters assert about reciprocal behavior by other countries and subjecting our countries to suits are overblown, especially given that existing exceptions under FSIA have been in place 40 years without any meaningful retaliation, or a flood of litigation against the United States. How do you feel about that?

Mr. EGAN. Congressman Conyers, I think we actually have seen some litigation in response to the terrorism exception, for example, where we are faced with default judgement from Iranian and Cuban courts in the billions of dollars in retaliatory action that they took in the 1990's and 2000's in response to our creating the terrorism exception.

We do face litigation overseas in the context of contracts and other activities that we would say foreign governments here are not immune from, and we vigorously defend ourselves in that litigation. The change here would be something that would be an additional exception that is not recognized by others in the world at this point, and that is why we are——

Mr. CONYERS. What impact has that had on us? Has it been minimal?

Mr. EGAN. I am sorry, sir. The litigation that we are currently facing?

Mr. CONYERS. The foreign judgments.

Mr. EGAN. So, for example, with respect to Iran and Cuba, in trying to resolve claims with those countries, including our own claims, these judgements are put forward by those countries as things that we must resolve before they will consider resolving our claims.

Of course, we believe very strongly that our claims have merit. Theirs do not, but they definitely become impediments in moving forward, including in collecting compensation for our property and other claims.

Mr. CONYERS. Ambassador Patterson, the bill supporters argue that if we enact this measure, it could help counterterrorism activities because it would help to deter future financing and other material support for terrorist attacks in the United States, and through enhanced public scrutiny of these countries that potentially may support terrorism. Do you think that that is a logical——

Ms. PATTERSON. I do not agree with that, Mr. Conyers, because I think what this would do—that suggests that the sources of these terrorist acts are countries like ours, where public transparency might have an impact, and I can assure you in many of the countries that I have served, that would not be an issue.

What I think it will do is limit our own freedom of action overseas as lawsuits proliferate in places like Pakistan and Egypt and other countries in the Middle East. So, I think it would reduce cooperation among countries, particularly in the Middle East, but also in South Asia, that work with us closely on counterterrorism activities.

Mr. CONYERS. Well, Madam Ambassador, what Nations might be concerned about exposure to possible litigation in American courts if this legislation were to become law?

Ms. PATTERSON. I think in American courts, I think there are a number of countries quite apart from Saudi Arabia that would be concerned about exposure in U.S. courts, and I think it would not only be related to the 9/11 attack. As I mentioned, we had potential terrorist attacks from Pakistan. We had potential terrorist attacks from Afghanistan. They could also be subject to this. We think the reach of this legislation is quite broad.

Mr. CONYERS. Thank you, Mr. Chairman.

Mr. FRANKS. And I thank the gentleman, and I now recognize Mr. Nadler for 5 minutes for questioning.

Mr. NADLER. Thank you, Mr. Chairman, for holding this hearing today. I have a number of questions, but I want to note that I am proud to be the lead Democratic sponsor of this bill, alongside Mr. King of New York. I represent Lower Manhattan, where thousands of Americans were brutally murdered in the September 11th, 2001, terrorist attacks. JASTA would help ensure that those responsible for aiding and abetting these attacks are held accountable for their actions.

Unfortunately, because of certain court decisions that misinterpreted the Foreign Sovereignty Immunities Act and the Antiterrorism Act, 9/11 victims and their families have been unable to pursue their claims in court against some of the parties they believe were responsible for funding the attacks.

JASTA simply reinstates what was understood to be the law for 30 years—that foreign states may be brought to justice for aiding and abetting acts of international terrorism that occur on American soil, whether or not the conduct that facilitated the attack was conducted in the United States.

Let me be clear—this bill does not prejudge the merits of any particular case. It simply ensures that the 9/11 families, or anyone else who may be similarly situated can plead their case in court.

We have various objection to this, and we will hear various objections to this legislation today, primarily centered around the fear that other Nations may pass reciprocal legislation in retaliation, which would subject Americans or the United States itself to liability in those countries.

I find this argument unpersuasive. Unless the United States engages in international terrorist activity, which is carefully defined in law, it would face no legal jeopardy if another country passed an identical law. And given that no countries have retaliated in the 40 years since the Foreign Sovereignty Immunities Act, and it's well established tort exception was enacted into law, it is hard to understand why this very narrow classification should now raise alarms.

To the extent that one particular country may fear being held to account for its actions and might be threatening retaliation of some sort, there is no—that is no reason to deny justice to the victims of 9/11 and their families.

The Foreign Sovereignty Immunities Act was intended in part to ensure that the President would not be put in the position of determining which claims could be heard, and which would be protected by sovereign immunity. Although JASTA enables the executive to stay court proceedings if it is engaging in good-faith diplomatic negotiations to resolve a claim, it places the final determination of legal claims in the courts, where it belongs.

JASTA is a narrow bill that has been carefully negotiated over the last 6 years and which passed the Senate unanimously for the second time in May. It deserves swift passage in the House of Representatives, as well, and I appreciate your holding this hearing today so that we can begin this process.

Now, Ambassador Egan—Mr. Egan, rather—I am sorry—as I understood your argument, if a foreign government writes a million-dollar check to Al-Qaeda in a café in New York to fund a terrorist attack in the United States, the existing tort exception to the Foreign Sovereign Immunities Act provides jurisdiction to sue that government in a U.S. court.

But if that same government agent wrote the same million-dollar check in a café in Geneva, his government should be immune from liability for causing the very same terrorist attack. What is the rationale for that argument?

Mr. EGAN. Thank you, Congressman. I think if we were to look back at the enactment of the tort exception that you referenced, I think that the legislative history shows that the focus and the driving force behind that exception was to allow for lawsuits against foreign governments in New York and in Washington, D.C., primarily, for activities that they took—that they undertook here in the United States.

Mr. NADLER. Right, but if a government—a foreign government—conspires with some international terrorist organization to conduct an attack in the United States, and writes the check to finance that activity in a café in New York, why should it be a different situation than if the same government conspires with the same international terrorist organization for the same attack but writes the check in London or Geneva? What is the difference?

Mr. EGAN. I think under that hypothetical, sir, if a foreign government were to take that clear of an action, I think we would have very clear grounds to designate them as state sponsors of terrorism, and they would be subjected to liability under that framework.

Mr. NADLER. If they were designated after the fact?

Mr. EGAN. Yes, if the reason for their designation was the act that is taking place in your hypothetical it would be liability.

Mr. NADLER. But what you are really saying is if they wrote the check in New York, they would be subject to legal action, and a court would determine the facts.

If they wrote the check in Geneva to finance the terrorist attack in New York, it would be up to the executive branch to make a political determination whether we wanted to designate them as a state sponsor of terrorism, which may be, A, fact-based, but B, politically determined, rather than leaving it—rather than having the court have jurisdiction to make the same determination, that it would, if the check was written in New York. What is the justification for that, and why should we stand for such a distinction?

Mr. EGAN. I think when the terrorism exception was passed in 1996, Congressman, it was passed because I think there was a recognition that national security and foreign policy decision-making must be worked into a process like this.

Mr. NADLER. Yes, but foreign policy decision-making presumably has the same considerations whether the foreign government wrote the check in New York or wrote the check in Geneva. Why the distinction that one has executive determination with possibly political and foreign policy considerations and the other is up to a court?

Mr. EGAN. I think that the state sponsor process, which is a fact-driven, intelligence-driven process——

Mr. NADLER. And politically driven.

Mr. EGAN [continuing]. Was seen as one that was the appropriate check that would allow for executive branch input into the process.

Mr. NADLER. Well, and the question is why there should be executive branch into the process depending on where the check was written for the same act, the same actors, et cetera. And my time has expired, unfortunately, because I have a number of other questions, but I will simply reserve that I do not think that that distinction makes much sense.

Mr. NADLER. I yield back.

Mr. FRANKS. I thank the gentleman, and I would also now like to thank Ambassador Patterson and Mr. Egan for their time and expertise. Thank you for coming, and I would like now to invite the members of our second panel of witnesses to come forward. While you are being seated, I will go ahead and introduce our witnesses.

Our first witness on this panel will be Michael Mukasey. From 2007 until 2009, Judge Mukasey served as the Attorney General of the United States, and from 1988 to 2006, he served as district judge in the United States District Court for the Southern District of New York, becoming Chief Judge in the year 2000.

Our next witness is Richard Klingler, a partner at Sidley Austin. Mr. Klingler has served as the general counsel and legal advisor on the National Security Council, and a special assistant and Senior Associate Council to the president.

Our third witness is Paul Stephan, the Jeffries distinguished professor of law at the University of Virginia Law School. Professor Stephan has served as counselor on international law, and at the U.S. Department of State, and as a law clerk to U.S. Supreme Court Justice Louis Powell.

Our final witness is Jimmy Gurulé, a professor of law at Norte Dame Law School. Professor Gurulé has served as the undersecretary for Enforcement at the Department of Treasury, and assistant attorney general for the Office of Justice Programs at the Justice Department. Thank you all for being here.

Each of the witnesses' written statements will be entered into the record in its entirety. And I would now ask that each witness summarize his or her testimony in 5 minutes or less, and to help you stay within that time, there is a timing light in front of you. The light switch will switch from green to yellow, indicating that you have 1 minute to conclude your testimony.

When the light turns red, it indicates that the witness' 5 minutes have expired. And before I recognize the witnesses, it is the tradition of the Subcommittee that they be sworn, so if you will please stand to be sworn.

Do you solemnly swear that the testimony that you are about to give will be the truth, the whole truth, and nothing but the truth, so help you God? Thank you, you may be seated. Let the record reflect that the witnesses answered in the affirmative.

And I will now recognize our first witness, Mr. Mukasey. Mr. Mukasey, welcome back, sir. And if you will please turn that microphone on before you speak.

TESTIMONY OF THE HONORABLE MICHAEL B. MUKASEY, OF COUNSEL, DEBEVOISE & PLIMPTON LLP

Mr. MUKASEY. Thank you, Mr. Chairman, and thanks to the ranking number, and thanks in particular to the Committee for having this hearing. I do not want to simply run through the statement that I submitted to the Committee; it is in the record.

I am particularly pleased to see that the Committee is holding this hearing because, you know, the founders thought that the Senate would be the saucer in which the passions that might be unleashed in the House would be cooled. This bill, as was pointed out earlier, went through the Senate by a voice vote with no hearing. So, it is a pleasure to see the House serving as the saucer that the founders thought the Senate would be.

There are two principal problems with this bill: one is reciprocity and the other is futility. Reciprocity, I think, has been an alluded to. It is not that it would open U.S. courts—that is, it would open liability of foreign governments in U.S. courts—it is that it would open U.S. personal overseas to retaliation overseas. We are the most present country in the world. We are in more places with more people than anybody else in the world; we are the only super-power in the world right now. We want to stay that way.

I think that passing a bill like this which chips away at the concept of sovereign immunity can only hurt us; because we are the most present country in the world, it cannot help us. And there are not only hostile countries, but friendly countries, where there are people who would like to see us held to account for things that they think we ought to be held to account for.

The former Secretary of Defense, Donald Rumsfeld, was threatened with prosecution in Belgium of all places, until it was pointed out that we could pull are NATO headquarters out of Brussels, and they came to their senses. There have been prosecutions of our armed forces in Italy; there are threats to do, as it was pointed out by the State Department, some of our people in Egypt were prosecuted in those courts.

And the courts in foreign countries, where people have an interest in doing this, are much less controlled, and much less fair than our own courts. And there is no indication necessarily that this would be limited to court proceedings, that they would pass an identical statute. They are going to use this as an excuse to chip away at sovereign immunity.

From what I can think of, there are only really two countries—three countries that have anything terrible to lose here. One is the United States, the other is the U.K., and the third is Israel. And those three countries have the most to lose from chipping away at that content.

As to futility, I cannot do really any better than Judge Royce Lamberth of the D.C. District Court in a case called in Iranian terrorism cases, in which he called those cases against Iran, which is already on the foreign terrorist sponsor list, unsustainable, because in essence, sovereign assets are not subjected to attachment; and what you create is essentially a bridge to nowhere.

This is not going to help the people it is intended to help. The only people I think it can help are trial lawyers. And I do not see passing a bill in aid of that.

I would also like to respond to a couple of questions that were raised in the course of the questioning before. One actually was in the initial comments of Chairman Goodlatte who said that, you know, if a foreign government gives a bomb to a terrorist organization, and they drop it, here, why should they not be subject to suit here? That is an act of war under any standard of international law. And when FDR went in front of Congress on December 8, 1941, he did not ask Congress to strip the sovereign immunity of Japan, and open it up to lawsuits for what they did at Pearl Harbor; he asked for a declaration of war.

There are obviously steps short of war that we can take, and those were outlined by the State Department. But that is the way we respond to conduct like that. As to the question of why it is that courts should not respond, I think Judge Lambert said specifically that courts are not suited to respond to this, and the Constitution says why courts should not respond.

The Constitution places in the hands of the executive the exclusive right to conduct foreign relations. It does not give it to Article III courts. And having been in an Article III court, I know that Article III courts take on a lot of reasonabilities, but I do not think that ought to be one. Thank you.

[The prepared statement of Mr. Mukasey follows:]

Testimony of Michael B. Mukasey

House of Representatives – Committee on the Judiciary

Subcommittee on the Constitution and Civil Justice

Chairman Franks, Ranking Member Cohen, and members of the Subcommittee. Thank you for inviting me to appear today to discuss S 2040, entitled the "Justice Against Sponsors of Terrorism Act." The bill tries to deal with some issues relating to the sovereign immunity of governments and their officials in the courts of the United States, and its title promises something that I think no one in this room, and indeed no decent person, would oppose as a matter of principle, and that is justice against those who sponsor acts of terrorism. However, for reasons I will outline, I believe that this bill and others like it would deliver far more harm to the United States, its officials and members of its military, and its interests generally, than it would deliver any justice to sponsors of terrorism or good to the citizens of this country.

In summary, although I think it is unlikely to achieve anything approaching justice for victims of terrorism, it is almost certain to invite retaliation against our own government officials, soldiers and diplomats, and to be used to justify proceedings against our allies, including but certainly not limited to Israel. For those reasons, I think it would be imprudent to pass it.

I have had the chance to deal with issues relating to terrorism, and to some extent with issues relating to sovereign immunity, during my career, including service as a U.S. District Judge for the Southern District of New York from 1988 to 2006, where I presided over several cases arising from the 1993 bombing of the World Trade Center in New York and related crimes, and later over cases arising from the attacks on 9/11 and other plots and acts that followed. I served as Attorney General of the United States from 2007 to 2009, when terrorism-related issues took up more of my time than any other single topic – literally from the opening daily briefing at FBI headquarters, and once a week at the White House, through the remainder of the day, including considering pending investigations, applications to the Foreign Intelligence Surveillance Court, and other issues presented by the war that has been launched against us by militant Islamists.

I have also written and spoken on these and related subjects since I left government in 2009. I have not been retained by anyone to appear here today. I am appearing on my own time and on my own dime because I am concerned at the negative effect I believe this bill would have on the interests of the United States and those of our allies.

I should say also at the outset that I am not a specialist in international law, and do not approach this legislation and this topic as a specialist. However, I have reviewed the testimony that was given before the Senate in July 2010 by John W. Bellinger III, who served as Legal Adviser for the State Department from 2005 to 2009, in addition to other positions he held earlier at the White House and in the Justice Department. In fact, he was serving as State Department Legal Adviser during the time that I served as Attorney General. He is a deservedly well respected specialist. I commend to your attention the testimony he gave exactly 6 years ago, on July 14, 2010, before the Subcommittee on

Crime and Drugs of the Senate Committee on the Judiciary. Although I may not agree with all the misgivings he expresses about legislation that is already on the books, I do share fully his misgivings about further legislation of the sort under consideration in 2010 and now, and I associate myself fully with his views.

There are, to be sure, technical problems with the legislation you are considering, and I will get to a couple of them later on. But the principal problems with this legislation are not technical. They arise from the simple fact that the United States is the most powerful nation in the world, and the nation most present in the world. It is most present in its diplomacy and in its military activities. I believe, and I think most of those in this room believe, that the United States is a force for good, one might even say the principal force for good – certainly compared to the other nations that seek to influence outcomes around the globe, including not only terrorist states like Iran but also adversaries like Russia and China.

This bill would invite retaliation by countries around the world, whether Turkey because of our support for the Kurds or Afghanistan because of death, or injury or property damage caused by drone strikes. Indeed, we have already seen threats of proceedings in friendly countries like Belgium and Spain against U.S. officials associated with acts that some in those countries disapprove of. It had to be pointed out to the Belgians that we could move NATO headquarters out of Brussels before they came to their senses and withdrew a threat to purport to exercise jurisdiction over our public officials. And we can certainly recall that there was a Spanish magistrate not long ago who suggested he could exercise what is known as universal jurisdiction and reach U.S. officials. All it would take would be one exception to sovereign immunity that we ourselves enact for a country hostile to U.S. interests to enact a statute purporting to impose liability on our officials, or those of our allies.

Do we really want members of our military who carry out lawful orders of their superiors subjected to punishment in foreign courts? Do we want that to happen to our diplomats? And make no mistake about it, there are public officials in foreign countries who would welcome our creating a breach in the wall of sovereign immunity that they could exploit to reach us, arguing that we are in no position to object.

It is not we alone who would be facing this danger. We would be weakening the doctrine of sovereign immunity for our allies as well, notably Israel. Israeli officials and members of its military have been threatened repeatedly with proceedings in foreign jurisdictions based on that country's acts in its own defense. The more exceptions we create to sovereign immunity, the more we endanger that country and its officials.

It also bears mention that there is already a law permitting actions against states that have been found by our executive to sponsor state terrorism, and there have been such actions, notably against Iran. Prevailing parties in some of those cases have judgments but have not collected on them because of obstacles thrown in the way by the Iranians. There is no assurance this bill would be any more successful.

As I mentioned before, there are technical issues with the legislation as well. The particular bill you are considering would create a new exception to the Foreign Sovereign Immunities Act for actions for money damages arising out of an act of international terrorism in the United States and "a tortious act . . . of the foreign state or of any official" acting anywhere in the world. The nature of the tortious act apparently need not itself constitute international terrorism. The bill purports to exclude from its reach and from the jurisdiction of U.S. courts "acts [by foreign countries and officials] that constitute mere negligence," although how that determination would be made without trying the case is impossible to imagine. In other words, under that bill, it would take a trial of the issue to determine whether the court had jurisdiction – a logical impossibility.

Further, the bill would permit a court to stay proceedings upon certification by the Secretary of State that good faith settlement negotiations are underway between the United States and the foreign state, with the implication that the United States government would have the authority to take settlement negotiations out of the hands of the plaintiffs in the litigation.

The technical problems with the bill, however, pale beside the overwhelming policy objection to it, and to any similar legislation, which is that it would obviously result in substantial harm to our public officials and members of our military, those of our allies, and therefore our own interests.

For the reasons outlined above, and in the July 14, 2010 testimony of John Bellinger, to which I referred earlier, HR 3815, or any similar legislation, should not be passed.

———————

Mr. FRANKS. Thank you, Judge Mukasey, and I would now recognize our second witness, Mr. Klingler. And, sir, if you would turn that microphone on.

TESTIMONY OF RICHARD D. KLINGLER, PARTNER, SIDLEY AUSTIN LLP

Mr. KLINGLER. Thank you, Chairman, Ranking Member Cohen for this opportunity to appear before you. My legal practice and service in government have focused on counterterrorism and related constitutional and statutory issues.

Although I represent certain victims of the September 11th attacks, in ongoing litigations that JASTA would assist, my comments address the broader benefits and operation of this important legislation, as elaborated in my written submission. JASTA modernizes the FSIA's treatment of claims directed against state-facilitated terrorism striking the United States.

As we painfully learned, terrorist attacks here are often the tragic conclusion of a course of conduct that originates abroad. Officials and agents of various foreign states in the Middle East, South and Central Asia and elsewhere, have various dealings with terrorist organizations, with international capabilities, and deeply-held hostility to Americans.

Courts have addressed state-facilitated terrorism under the FSIA for decades, but risks of adverse state action are increasing. At the same time, our Nation's capabilities to address these risks through civil litigation have proven inadequate. The principal statute designed to deter and remedy acts of terrorism, the ATA, generally does not apply to foreign states.

Two FSIA provisions already permit certain terrorism-related claims against foreign states, but one depends on the rarely used power to designate foreign states sponsors of terrorism, and the other, the tort exception, is not designed for terrorism in particular, and has at times has been applied narrowly.

JASTA enhances the ability of U.S. courts to address acts of terrorism, but only narrowly expands existing exceptions to foreign sovereign immunity. It slightly adjusts the tort exception, which has long supported claims against state-sponsored terrorism.

JASTA supports only claims that concern a state facilitated attack on U.S. soil. Any sovereign has the ability and obligation to remedy such injuries; as the Supreme Court cases made clear, Congress is the appropriate body to discharge that obligation, by enabling legal claims.

Expanding the scope of civil litigation can ensure justice for victims, deter and redress specific attacks and enhance our Nation's counterterrorism efforts. The prospect of litigation can prompt sovereigns to disentangle their operations from terrorist networks, or to provide justice to victims. Judicial processes, or state-to-state negotiated settlements, can provide a reckoning with history, demonstrate current commitment to right conduct, and enhance relationships with the U.S. government and financial community.

JASTA also claims the FSIA's strategy of depoliticizing immunity determination by transferring responsibility from the executive to the judiciary, but it maintains important roles for the executive. JASTA does not disturb the president's exclusive role to determine which foreign states maybe subject to sue for claims of injury abroad.

For terrorist attacks here, JASTA draws upon a different presidential power, to suspend claims to effectuate state-to-state agreements that would provide comparable redress. For claims under Section 1605(b), the executive can limit suits against foreign sovereigns, but must do so while also fostering the interest of the victims. Nor does the possibility that foreign states might mirror JASTA's jurisdiction pose risk to U.S. activities.

JASTA narrowly focuses on state-facilitated acts of international terrorism, based on a narrow, established definition. Its exception does not extend to self-defense and like actions, and does not concern claims against individuals.

If the concern is instead that foreign states will use JASTA simply as an excuse to implement broader exceptions to immunity, that has little to do with JASTA. Any state seeking to do so could point to the FSIA's existing tort exception, and its provisions related to state-sponsored terrorism.

As the Supreme Court Salman Khan decision confirms, the FSIA and JASTA's amendments, therefore, have nothing to do with claims against individual officials, and provide no basis for foreign states to expand claims against American officials. The scope of sovereignty administered by the executive is unchanged with respect to those individuals.

But the relative exception to sovereignty related to claims against foreign states was created in 1976, and expanded in the 1980's and 1990's. JASTA is no sea change. Its opponent's real quarrel is with Congress' earlier policy judgements, which have produced no dire consequences over decades.

Instead, considerations of military, political and economic power, and our diplomacy, have determined, and will continue to determine, whether foreign Nations foster legal claims against the United States, just as they do for other potential foreign state actions adverse to our interests. JASTA would not change that calculus.

It does, though, empower and encourage our diplomats to use those traditional tools more effectively, to include the interests of victims of terrorism among our highest foreign policy objectives.

And if I might add just a quick observation about the State Department presentations we just heard—you know, they failed to acknowledge how existing FSIA provisions could be used as the pretext for expanded foreign state jurisdiction that the State Department fears. They failed to point to any adverse consequences arisen from decades of cases applying 1605, 85 and Section 1605A, to foreign states for facilitating terror, other than the Cuban and Iranian judgments, which frankly are a political issue, and would be dealt with on a political basis just as any others would.

The Department failed to note that the Administration's own prominent exaggerations of the changes reflected in JASTA have contributed to certain confusion and discomfort on the issue abroad.

And it failed to address, altogether, the Department's role in fostering state-to-state settlements and securing accountability for wrongful foreign state actions directed at U.S. citizens.

All these characteristics of the Department's response indicate why JASTA is needed, rather than why it is not, and explains why the Senate unanimously rejected the Administration's arguments. So JASTA confirms Congresses' initial policy judgments reflecting the FFSI, and generally seeks to ensure the Department will place a much higher priority on terrorism. Thank you.

[The prepared statement of Mr. Klingler follows:]

"The Justice Against Sponsors of Terrorism Act"

**Hearing Before the House Judiciary Committee,
Subcommittee on the Constitution and Civil Justice**

July 14, 2016

**Richard Klingler
Partner, Sidley Austin LLP**

Statement of Richard Klingler

**Before the House Judiciary Committee, Subcommittee on the Constitution and Civil
Justice**

"The Justice Against Sponsors of Terrorism Act"

July 14, 2016

Thank you Mr. Chairman and Ranking Member Cohen for this opportunity to address S.

2040, the Justice Against Sponsors of Terrorism Act – or "JASTA." I am a partner in the law

firm Sidley Austin LLP with a practice focusing on constitutional law, administrative law, and

national security matters. I served as Senior Associate Counsel and Special Assistant to

President George W. Bush, as the Legal Adviser on the staff of the National Security Council,

and, much earlier, as a law clerk to Justice Sandra Day O'Connor. Although I represent certain

of the victims of the attacks of September 11, 2001 in asserting their claims against particular

foreign states and other facilitators of terrorism, claims that JASTA would assist, my comments

are directed generally toward the broader benefits and operation of this important legislation.

JASTA modernizes and addresses gaps in the Foreign Sovereign Immunities Act's

treatment of claims in U.S. courts directed against terrorism striking the United States and

facilitated by officials and agents of foreign states. As we have painfully learned in this century,

terrorist attacks are often the tragic conclusion of a course of conduct that originates abroad and

ends in the United States. We also have learned that officials and agents of various foreign states

have a broad range of dealings with terrorist organizations with international capabilities and

deeply held hostility to the United States and Americans. With or without the support of the

highest officials of various states in the Middle East, South and Central Asia, and portions of

Southeast Asia and Northern Africa, lesser officials and agents of these foreign states have, at

47

times, facilitated the development or directly assisted the terrorist activities of some of the world's most dangerous terrorist organizations. This phenomenon is not entirely new: since the 1970s, courts have entertained claims directed against efforts by foreign governments as different as Chile and the Republic of China to harm persons in the United States, often dissidents or expatriates seeking refuge here. Even so, the multitude of state-affiliated persons and entities supporting terrorist organizations, and the scale of the damage those organizations seek to cause here, are far different and require a far more robust response.

Even as these threats associated with foreign states have grown, our nation's capabilities to address them through civil litigation have decreased or proved inadequate. The principal federal statute intended to deter and provide redress for acts of terrorism, the Anti-Terrorism Act, generally cannot be invoked against foreign states and their officials. Terrorism-related claims against foreign sovereigns are facilitated by two provisions of the Foreign Sovereign Immunities Act (FSIA): Section 1605A, which permits suits against foreign states designated by the State Department as state sponsors of terrorism, and Section 1605(a)(5), the non-commercial tort exception to immunity.[1] Section 1605A requires an all-or-nothing determination whether a foreign state is amenable to suit, and a designation carries with it a range of commerce and other restrictions that extend far beyond expanding a state's amenability to suit. For this reason and the broader diplomatic implications of the designation, the State Department has been reluctant to impose the designation on foreign states whose officials have facilitated or do facilitate terrorism but that also cooperate with the United States at times. As a result, only Sudan, Syria, and Iran are currently designated as state sponsors of terrorism, and current policy calls into question whether even those designations will persist. Cuba and North Korea, for example, have

---

[1] 28 U.S.C. §§ 1605(a)(5) & 1605A.

been dropped from the list of designees. As for Section 1605(a)(5), certain courts have narrowed the scope of that provision, for example by excluding from its reach acts undertaken abroad that would otherwise meet the statutory requirements of causing "damage in the United States" or by limiting the acts attributable to the foreign state.

Enhancing the ability of U.S. courts to address claims against the sponsors of terrorism directed toward the United States, including those affiliated with foreign states, advances three central interests: ensuring justice for the victims of terrorism, deterring and redressing specific attacks within the nation's boundaries, and, more broadly, enhancing our nation's counter-terrorism efforts. Civil litigation is a relatively small but still important component of our counter-terrorism capabilities. As U.S. courts have repeatedly emphasized, the threat of civil penalties and associated public scrutiny can serve as an important deterrent for state organizations and affiliated persons, often of significant wealth or public stature, who might otherwise finance or enable terrorist activities. This deterrent effect may be especially important for prompting foreign sovereigns to ensure that officials at all levels of government, including regulators and quasi-governmental organizations, confront rather than assist terrorist organizations. Foreign sovereigns and their associated organizations have an important responsibility and unique capability to provide redress, accountability, and justice for the victims of terrorism. And, judicial processes – or a comparable state-to-state negotiated settlement – have important potential foreign policy benefits for the foreign state defendant and the United States. Those processes enable the foreign state to set history right with respect to the acts of prior officials, to demonstrate its current and prospective commitment to confronting terrorism, and to enhance its relationship with the U.S. government and financial community.

JASTA responds to the problems posed by modern state-sponsored terrorism and
achieves the broader objectives -- of justice, defense, and enhanced counter-terrorism --
associated with facilitating civil litigation directed toward terrorist acts. It does this through
three principal mechanisms:

- JASTA would add a new provision of the Foreign Sovereign Immunities Act, Section
  1605B.[2] That provision confirms that claims may proceed against sovereigns that
  facilitate a terrorist attack on U.S. soil, even if that facilitation occurred through acts
  undertaken abroad. It also confirms that state sovereigns will be held liable for the acts
  of their agents and for a broad range of tortious conduct that facilitates terrorism.

- The Act would extend the scope of the Anti-Terrorism Act ("ATA").[3] As amended, the
  ATA would authorize claims against foreign officials for facilitating acts of international
  terrorism, to the extent that the claim also falls within the scope of the new Section
  1605B. The Act also clarifies that liability arises under the ATA for various forms of
  assistance, including aiding and abetting and conspiracy, that facilitate a foreign terrorist
  organization's actions harming U.S. persons. The ATA defines the scope of relevant
  tortious conduct in the terrorism context.

- JASTA also seeks to facilitate the state-to-state resolution of terrorism-related claims and
  to coordinate judicial claims with the Executive Branch's foreign policy initiatives.[4] It
  does so by providing that actions maintained under the new Section 1605B may be stayed
  upon a certification by the Secretary of State that the United States is engaged in good

---

[2] S. 2040, 114th Cong., 2d Sess., § 3.

[3] *Id.* § 4.

[4] *Id.* § 5.

faith negotiations to have the foreign state defendant provide redress to the affected victims of terrorism.

JASTA carefully tailors the scope of newly enabled claims to address the legal and practical challenges to our nation's counter-terrorism efforts outlined above. Section 1605B enables only claims that seek redress for injury caused by an act of international terrorism, defined by reference to an existing and well understood statutory provision – and supplemented by a further limitation that excludes acts of war.[5] That injury is further limited to "physical injury to person or property or death."[6] Perhaps most significantly, the injury forming the basis of the claim must occur in the United States.[7] And, it must be caused by certain types of tortious acts undertaken by officials or agents associated with a foreign state or otherwise attributable to the state. Allegations of omissions or mere negligence by the foreign state officials cannot provide the basis for recovery.[8] And good faith, state-to-state negotiations between the United States and the defendant state to remedy the harm underlying the claims may suspend court proceedings.

With respect to terrorism-related claims, the new Section 1605B in large measure simply restores and moderately adjusts the scope for claims authorized by the text of the non-commercial tort exception to sovereign immunity, subsection 1605(a)(5).[9] That subsection provides an exception to immunity for claims seeking damages "against a foreign state for

---

[5] *Id.* § 3 (Section1605B(a)).

[6] *Id.* (Section 1605B(b)).

[7] *Id.*

[8] *Id.* (Section 1605B(d)).

[9] 28 U.S.C. § 1605(a)(5).

personal injury or death, or damage to or loss of property," limited to injury "occurring in the United States" and "caused by the tortious act" of a "foreign state or of any official or employee of that foreign state while acting within the scope of his office or employment."[10] Section 1605(a)(5)'s terms are more expansive than that of Section 1605B to the extent that the existing provision permits claims based on omissions and negligence and is not limited to injury caused by acts of international terrorism. Section 1605(a)(5) is somewhat more limited than Section 1605B in its exclusion of certain claims related to the discretionary functions of state officials and commercial activities and distinct torts that have little relation to terrorism. Section 1605B confirms that the acts of a state's agent can give rise to liability and, perhaps most importantly, confirms that claims can be based on acts of the foreign state committed abroad, as long as they contribute to injury in the United States. Likewise, the amendment to the ATA rejects narrowing judicial constructions that disallow recovery based on claims of secondary liability – for example, aiding and abetting through the provision of material support for terrorism, or conspiring with others who commit the terrorist act.[11]

Similarly, Section 1605B can be viewed as redressing the implementation weaknesses that have bedeviled Section 1605A – at least for injury occurring from an act of terrorism in the United States. Section 1605A similarly focuses on claims seeking damages for injury caused by acts of terrorism undertaken with a foreign state's support. Unlike Section 1605B, which extends only to injury occurring in the United States (without regard to the nationality of the injured claimant), Section 1605A lifted immunity for claims based on terrorism-related injury occurring anywhere in the world – but only for injury to U.S. persons. More importantly,

---

[10] *Id.*

[11] S. 2040, *supra*, § 4.

52

Section 1605A operates only against persons affiliated with sovereigns that the U.S. government has deemed to be state sponsors of terrorism. As described above, this dependence on Executive Branch action has proved quite unsatisfactory and has resulted in a very limited scope for terrorism-related claims against sovereigns. JASTA's separate provision permitting courts to stay claims asserted by victims of terrorism where the Executive is negotiating state-to-state settlements establishes a separate and more comprehensive mechanism for coordinating the assessments of Congress and the Executive.

Three principal objections have been directed toward JASTA: that Congress has done too much, by addressing matters more appropriately left to the Executive Branch; that Congress has done too little, because it has left resolution of claims to the judicial process; and that JASTA will prompt foreign states to facilitate legal claims directed against the United States. Especially when set against the benefits secured by JASTA, noted above, these objections have little merit.

a.   First, the objection that Congress is invading the province of the President is quite misdirected. Congress has an entirely legitimate and, indeed, primary role in defining the scope of a foreign state's immunity in U.S. courts. Contrary to the occasionally expressed view that the Executive is the nation's "sole organ" in foreign affairs (which, more properly, means at most the sole organ in communicating with foreign nations), Congress and the President in fact share responsibility for formulating and directing the nation's foreign relations. Congress's powers arise from the Constitution's commitment to Congress or to the Senate of powers over foreign commerce, spending, "defin[ing] and punish[ing] ... Offenses against the Law of

Nations," consenting to treaties and appointments of diplomats, and controlling various domestic matters that bear on our foreign relations.[12]

More specifically, as the Supreme Court has described, "[b]y reason of its authority over foreign commerce and foreign relations, Congress has the undisputed power to decide, as a matter of federal law, whether and under what circumstances foreign nations should be amenable to suit in the United States."[13] Supreme Court cases extending back to 1812 have established that no foreign state is entitled to any exclusion from the jurisdiction of our federal courts, because "the jurisdiction of a nation within its own territory 'is susceptible of no limitation not imposed upon itself.'"[14] Congress has taken the lead in defining the scope of sovereign immunity since the passage of the Foreign Sovereign Immunities Act of 1976. In "[e]nacting the FSIA in 1976, Congress transferred from the Executive to the courts the principal responsibility for determining a foreign state's amenability to suit," and "it remains Congress' prerogative to alter a foreign state's immunity and to render the alteration dispositive of judicial proceedings in progress."[15] The just-quoted decision illustrates the scope of Congress's power: there, the Supreme Court upheld a revision to the FSIA's provisions that was directed against a single sovereign (Iran) and which affected a single, consolidated judicial proceeding.

JASTA reflects Congress's leading role in defining foreign sovereign immunity but still seeks to advance the national interest by coordinating Congressional, judicial, and Executive

---

[12] U.S. Const., Art. I, § 8; *see Bank Markazi v. Peterson*, 136 S.Ct. 1310, 1328 (2016); *Zivotofsky v. Kerry*, 135 S.Ct. 2076, 2087 (2015).

[13] *Verlinden B.V. v. Central Bank of Nigeria*, 461 U.S. 480, 493 (1983).

[14] *Id.* at 482 (quoting *The Schooner Exchange v. M'Faddon*, 7 Cranch 116, 136 (1812) (Marshall, C.J.)); *see also Republic of Austria v. Altmann*, 541 U.S. 677, 688 (2004).

[15] *Bank Markazi v. Peterson*, 136 S.Ct. at 1329 (2016); *id.* (citing *Republic of Iraq v. Beaty*, 556 U.S. 848, 856-57, 865 (2009)).

Branch efforts to address claims against foreign states. For claims in U.S. courts addressing terrorism-related injuries to U.S. persons occurring abroad, JASTA does not disturb the President's exclusive role under Section 1605A to determine which foreign states may be subject to suit. Claims may proceed against only those foreign states that the President, through the Secretary of State, has designated as state sponsors of terrorism. However, for claims against foreign states associated with acts of terror causing harm within the United States, JASTA draws upon a different Presidential power to ensure that the branches of government are coordinated. The President has the power at least to suspend claims against foreign states in U.S. courts to effectuate state-to-state agreements that would provide comparable, alternative redress to the affected claimants.[16] JASTA recognizes and enhances this power by providing that claims against foreign states related to domestic terrorism may be suspended if the Secretary of State certifies that the Executive Branch is engaged in good faith negotiations with the foreign state defendant to secure alternative redress for the claimants.

JASTA's additional coordination mechanism appropriately does not rely completely on Executive Branch determinations. For cases involving injury within the United States, the Act does not permit the Executive to shield a sovereign from suit altogether but instead enables the Executive to affect particular cases, but only if the Executive and the foreign state defendant are engaged in good faith negotiations to provide a remedy to the claimants. That strategy continues the process initiated by the FSIA of depoliticizing the immunity determination. Before the passage of the FSIA, under the processes administered and formalized by the State Department beginning in 1952, "foreign nations often placed diplomatic pressure on the State Department in seeking immunity. On occasion, political considerations led to suggestions of immunity in cases

---

[16] *See Dames & Moore v. Regan*, 453 U.S. 654 (1981); *see also Amer. Ins. Ass'n v. Garamendi*, 539 U.S. 396 (2003).

where immunity would not [otherwise] have been available ... ."[17] As a result, Congress passed the FSIA "to free the Government from the case-by-case diplomatic pressures, to clarify the governing standards, and to 'assure litigants that ... decisions are made purely on legal grounds and under procedures that insure due process.'"[18] Or, more bluntly, "Congress abated th[is] bedlam in 1976, replacing the old executive-driven, factor intensive, loosely common-law-based immunity regime with the Foreign Sovereign Immunities Act's 'comprehensive set of legal standards governing claims of immunity in every civil action against a foreign state.'"[19] The addition of Section 1605A to the FSIA, relying on the Executive Branch's discretionary determinations of which foreign states would be amenable to suit for certain terrorism-related claims, reflected a partial return to the pre-1976 model of deference to the State Department -- and brought along with it the political pressures and process defects that the FSIA had been designed to eliminate. JASTA reverses that departure for a subset of terrorism-related cases and returns to an approach more in keeping with the broader structure and operation of the FSIA.

Litigation undertaken by the victims of the September 11, 2001 attacks against the Kingdom of Saudi Arabia, various prominent Saudi financiers of terrorism, and others illustrate how the Executive Branch responds to this type of political pressure in particular cases. The Department of Justice had, during a previous Administration, assured the courts that, under its construction of the FSIA, suits against foreign states alleged to have facilitated the September

---

[17] *Verlinden B.V. v. Central Bank of Nigeria*, 461 U.S. at 487.

[18] *Id.*, 461 U.S. at 488 (quoting H.R. Rep. No. 94-1487, p. 7 (1976)).

[19] *Repub. of Argentina v. NML Capital, Ltd.*, 134 S.Ct. 2250, 2255 (2014) (quoting *Verlinden B.V. v. Central Bank of Nigeria*, 461 U.S. at 488).

11th attacks could proceed in U.S. courts.[20] Later, however, when required to address an actual

case of this type, the Department acted quite differently. It disregarded its own earlier reasoning

and instead strained to present prior cases and the FSIA itself as precluding claims against the

Kingdom or as otherwise indicating that the U.S. Supreme Court should not undertake to review

decisions adverse to the victims of the September 11th attacks.[21] It sought to block claims by the

victims even when the Department publicly acknowledged that the courts below had dismissed

the claims based on basic *misconstructions* of the FSIA (mistakes later recognized even by the

lower court below).[22] Likewise, the Administration has not acted consistently with assurances

that it had provided to representatives of the victims of the attacks regarding how the government

would address and advance their claims. Similarly, the Administration's extensive negotiations

with Iran have apparently not included any effort to ensure that Iran satisfy the billions of dollars

in damages that victims of Iranian-sponsored terrorism, including the victims of the September

11th attacks, have had recognized in judgments entered by U.S. courts against Iran. Throughout,

the Administration has advocated for foreign states, including states quite hostile to American

---

[20] Brief for *Amicus Curiae*, United States, in Support of Plaintiffs-Appellees, No. 03-7117, at p. 17, *Kilburn v. Libyan Arab Jamahiriya*, 376 F.3d 1123 (D.C. Cir. 2004) ("For example, in cases of terrorism on U.S. territory, such as the September 11 attacks, jurisdiction might properly be founded on both paragraphs (a)(5) and (a)(7).").

[21] *See* Brief of the United States as *Amicus Curiae*, *Federal Ins. Co. v. Kingdom of Saudi Arabia*, No. 08-640 (U.S. Supreme Court, June 1, 2009); Supplemental Brief of Petitioners in Response to the United States, *Federal Ins. Co. v. Kingdom of Saudi Arabia*, No. 08-640 (U.S. Supreme Court, June 8, 2009); *see also* Brief of the United States as *Amicus Curiae*, *In re Terrorist Attacks of September 11, 2001, O'Neill v. Al Rajhi Bank*, No. 13-318 (U.S. Supreme Court, May 27, 2014); Supplemental Brief of Petitioners in Response to the Brief of the United States, *In re Terrorist Attacks of September 11, 2001, O'Neill v. Al Rajhi Bank*, No. 13-318 (U.S. Supreme Court, June 9, 2014).

[22] *See* Brief of the United States as *Amicus Curiae*, *Federal Ins. Co. v. Kingdom of Saudi Arabia*, *supra*, at pp. 6-8, 13-15.

interests, and has advanced those states' interests at the expense of the victims of the most significant terrorist attack on U.S. soil.

b.   A different objection is that Congress should do more than JASTA accomplishes, and instead should directly assess whether particular claims against a foreign state are meritorious and, if so, should then enable recovery from the sovereign's assets located in the United States.

How Congress might effectively and fairly undertake such assessments or provide for recovery is entirely unclear. Congress has, for example, extensively examined facts related to the persons and entities that contributed to the growth of al Qaeda and to the September 11th attacks,[23] but those conclusions were not designed to function as the equivalent of judicial determinations or to provide the basis for proceeding against any foreign sovereign's assets. Arranging for the freezing and disposition of U.S.-based assets would require processes associated with the sanctions regimes or wartime measures, and would be highly inflammatory and destabilizing. Nor are making such liability-related determinations and providing for related recovery, other than through the judicial process, usual functions of Congress or traditionally employed in having foreign sovereigns redress injuries caused in the United States. Any such effort would be perceived, with some justification, as more politicized and less consistent with due process principles than comparable determinations of liability and measures to compel payment carried out by courts of law using generally applicable legal principles and processes.

Instead, JASTA appropriately make use of the same judicial mechanisms, and the same allocation of powers between Congress and the judiciary, that the FSIA has employed for the

---

[23] *See, e.g., Joint Inquiry into Intelligence Community Activities Before and After the Terrorist Attacks of September 11, 2001*, Report of the U.S. Senate Select Comm. on Intelligence and U.S. House Permanent Select Comm. on Intelligence, S. Rept. No. 107-351, H. Rept. 107-792, 107th Cong., 2d Sess. (Dec. 2002).

past forty years. Congress defines when a foreign sovereign may be amenable to suit in federal court, but any liability on the part of a foreign state arises under generally applicable state and federal laws and is determined in contested proceedings before independent judges while affording all the procedural protections to the foreign sovereign that are afforded to other litigants in U.S. courts, domestic or foreign. Congress has no obligation to assume the judicial function, and all the benefits secured by the FSIA counsel against doing so. Again, that statute was designed "to free the Government from the case-by-case diplomatic pressures, to clarify the governing standards, and to 'assure litigants that … decisions are made purely on legal grounds and under procedures that insure due process,'"[24] and all those benefits would be lost if Congress were to resolve and provide specific remedies related to individual claims against foreign states.

        c.   Finally, some raise concerns that certain foreign states may respond to JASTA by authorizing reciprocal suits directed against legitimate actions of this nation abroad. Although the risk of overreaching foreign suits has long existed and will continue to need to be monitored and addressed, JASTA does not give rise to or increase that risk.

To the extent the concern is that other foreign states will replicate the jurisdiction afforded by JASTA, that result would pose no risk to legitimate U.S. activities. JASTA is narrowly focused on state-facilitated acts of international terrorism and explicitly excludes from its scope any exception to immunity for acts of war, omissions, and mere negligence. JASTA's reference to "international terrorism" relies directly on a narrow, well-defined definition that is long-embedded in U.S. law and addressed by decades of judicial decisions. The Act confirms that its exception to immunity does not extend to military, self-defense, and other initiatives that this nation properly uses to defend its interests.

---

[21] *See supra* n.18.

If the concern is instead that foreign states will use JASTA as an excuse to implement *broader* exceptions to immunity that could impede U.S. activities, then that concern has little to do with JASTA. The FSIA's non-commercial tort exception and especially its provisions related to state-sponsored terrorism, such as Section 1605A, already provide the ostensible basis for any foreign state seeking to facilitate litigation against the United States. And even if the FSIA did not already contain such provisions, it would be perverse to decline to defend our legitimate interests in resisting state-sponsored terrorism simply because we feared that our adversaries would mislabel our legitimate self-defense efforts as "international terrorism."

Those pressing this concern also mistake diplomatic issues for legal ones. Lawyers, especially international lawyers, often exaggerate the legal component of what are essentially issues of economic, political, and military power to be addressed in the context of bilateral and multilateral relations. Those considerations of power, and our diplomacy, are what will cause foreign nations to decline or seek to facilitate illegitimate legal claims against the United States, just as those factors affect whether foreign states might undertake any other actions that would be adverse to our interests. JASTA provides foreign states with no legitimate argument that would change this calculus. To the extent that the real concern is, instead, that particular foreign states would not relish being held to account for their facilitation of acts of international terrorism visited upon the United States, then those same, broader factors come into play and our diplomats have an opportunity to ensure that victims of terrorism secure justice even as foreign nations are encouraged to assist rather than evade our nation's counter-terrorism efforts.

Thank you for your attention, and I would be pleased to respond to any questions you may have.

———————

Mr. FRANKS. I thank you gentlemen. And I would now recognize our third witness, Mr. Stephan. And, Mr. Stephan, if you would please turn that microphone on.

TESTIMONY OF PAUL B. STEPHAN, PROFESSOR OF LAW, UNIVERSITY OF VIRGINIA LAW SCHOOL

Mr. STEPHAN. Thank you, Mr. Chairman Franks, Ranking Member Mr. Cohen, and other Members of the Committee; I am very grateful for the opportunity to testify here. I have devoted my entire professional life to the foreign relations law of the United States, both in the academy and in government service. I have no clients; I represent no one in this case. I am here to try and help the Committee if I can.

I speak in opposition to the bill under consideration. I wish to make three points. First, this bill, were it adopted as law, would likely harm the United States, as well as our allies by increasing exposure to litigation abroad.

Second, this bill is not likely to achieve its stated aim, which is to whole foreign states accountable for material support for terrorism and to provide justice for their victims.

Third, this bill would privatize the national security of the United States, contrary to any sensible antiterrorism policy.

Existing law already provides a right for victims of state-sponsored terrorism to seek compensation through litigation. What this bill would do is strip the executive branch of its proper authority, provided by this Congress, to determine which states sponsor terrorism, and to give that power instead to private litigants. Such a grave matter as identifying states that are mortal threats to U.S. interests should not be left to private lawsuits. To put it bluntly, if Saudi Arabia did provide material support for the 9/11 attacks, we should be responding with cruise missiles, not with plaintiff's attorneys.

And if they did not, seeking to extract money from them for the victims of those attacks may be justified on principals of charity and compassion, but not by justice. As you already have heard today, no country benefits from the international law of sovereign immunity more than the United States.

Moreover, our worldwide interests and responsibilities mean that we do many things that foreign lawyers and judges do not like, and might consider illegal, especially when we fight terrorism. At the end of the day, increasing the exposure of our antiterrorism effort to foreign legal liability does not seem like a sound way to fight terrorist threats.

Let me make this point concrete—in response to the judgement of the International Court of Justice requiring sovereign immunity, the Italian courts proved defiant. They struck down an act of their Parliament that had implemented this judgement, declaring that the rights of persons to litigate their claims in Italian courts overrides core principals of international law.

Italy, as already has been noted today, is also a country where courts have brought criminal prosections against U.S. officials involved in apprehending suspected terrorists. These prosecutions arguably violate Italy's treaty commitments to us. Enactment of this bill will encourage the Italian courts, already inclined to disregard specific rules of international law, as well as treaties, to create even more exceptions to sovereign immunities. This would expose the United States to severe litigation risks for counterterrorism activates.

Other countries will notice and respond accordingly, not only against us, but against our allies in this struggle, including the United Kingdom and Israel.

Next, it is very unlikely that this bill will achieve its stated purpose. Most states, when confronted with lawsuits in foreign courts that they regard as violating their rights under international law, refuse to appear. When default judgements result, they refuse to pay. This bill does not affect the incentives of foreign states to do exactly this.

As a result, the lawsuits the bill would permit are unlikely to unearth evidence that would identify, much less punish, state sponsors of terrorism, or to produce acknowledgement of culpability accompied by compensation.

Finally, there is something seriously wrong with privatizing American national security policy. Although Section 5 of the Senate bill allows the judge to stay the suit at the request of the executive, it does not require this. It still leaves it to the court and the litigants to decide when to do so. If they regard the efforts of the executive to unearth evidence of state support for terrorism is unsatisfactory, this bill gives them a green light to go forward.

It is therefore completely unlike the Iranian claims litigation, where the executive could require courts to stay lawsuits. Thank you for your attention; I am happy to take questions.

[The prepared statement of Mr. Stephan follows:]

Statement of Paul B. Stephan, University of Virginia, before a Hearing of the House Judiciary Committee's Subcommittee on the Constitution and Civil Justice on S. 2040, the "Justice Against Sponsors of Terrorism Act" on July 14, 2016

Good morning. My name is Paul Stephan, and I am the John C. Jeffries, Jr., Distinguished Professor of Law and the John V. Ray Research Professor of Law at the University of Virginia. I have been teaching and writing about the foreign relations law of the United States for all of my 37 years on the Virginia faculty. I served as Counselor for International Law to the Legal Adviser of the Department of State in 2006-2007, where I worked on many sovereign immunity issues. Currently I am a coordinating reporter for the American Law Institute's Fourth Restatement of the Foreign Relations Law of the United States, which includes sovereign immunity. I appear here on my own behalf, and nothing I say should be taken as representing the views of the University of Virginia School of Law, the State Department, or the American Law Institute. I have no clients with any interest in this proposed legislation and represent no one. Rather, I am here before you in the role of a disinterested student of foreign relations law who hopes to help this body in its deliberations.

I speak here in opposition to the bill under consideration (JASTA). I wish to make three points. First, this bill, were it adopted as law, would likely harm the United States by increasing its exposure to litigation abroad. Second, this bill is not likely to achieve its stated aim, which is to hold foreign states accountable for material support for terrorism and to provide justice for their victims. Third, this bill would privatize the national security of the United States, contrary to any sensible antiterrorism policy. Existing law already provides a right for victims of state-sponsored terrorism to seek compensation through litigation. What this bill would do is strip the Executive Branch of its proper authority, as provided by this Congress, to determine which states sponsor terrorism and give that power instead to private litigants. Such a grave matter as identifying states that are mortal threats to U.S. interests should not be left to private lawsuits.

It probably needs no saying – but I will say anyway – that the plight of victims of terrorism, most significantly those of the 9/11 attacks, demands our deepest sympathy and should engage our greatest efforts to see that they get justice. These people suffered death and awful injuries, and their families terrible loss, for nothing more than showing up to do their job. If I thought that this bill would bring justice to those families, I would vigorously support it. My concern is that the bill will not do this, and might instead sow the seeds of future threats to our people as well as harm our country's interests.

States have enjoyed immunity from lawsuits in the courts of other states since the foundation of the modern international legal system in the seventeenth century. Chief Justice Marshall, writing for the Supreme Court, recognized this principle as a matter of U.S. law in 1812. He observed that the "common interest impelling [sovereign states] to mutual intercourse, and an interchange of good offices with each other," requires this exemption from judicial jurisdiction.[1] Only a few years ago, in Germany versus Italy, the International Court of Justice confirmed the broad principle that international law requires all nations to immunize foreign states from litigation in their courts, absent a few

---

[1] Schooner Exchange v. M'Faddon, 11 U.S. (7 Cranch) 116, 137 (1812).

narrow exceptions.[2] In particular, that Court ruled that a state could not allow private litigants to haul a foreign sovereign into court simply by alleging violations of international law, even grave human rights abuses. States always can waive this immunity, in particular instances or by treaty. But international law does not allow them to be forced into another country's courts against their will, except in a few narrow circumstances not applicable here.

No country benefits from this rule of international law more than does the United States. On the one hand, our extensive international engagements mean that we have property around the world that might be vulnerable to the execution of foreign judgments. I have not run the numbers, but I suspect that, given the extent of our global commitments and activities, the United States has more exposure to shrinkage of sovereign immunity than any other country. On the other hand, our worldwide interests and responsibilities mean that we do many things that foreign lawyers and judges do not like and might consider illegal. Over the past few years, suits in foreign courts against the United States have multiplied. Only the international legal regime of sovereign immunity protects us from serious material risk as well as distracting harassment.

JASTA erodes this protection. If enacted, it will be seen around the world as a clear violation of international law, as well as a bid to change that law to diminish immunity. You must remember that a breach of international law occurs as soon as a lawsuit commences, not when judgment is issued. Unlike the current terrorism exception in U.S.

---

[2] Jurisdictional Immunities of the State (Germany v. Italy), Judgment (Feb. 3, 2012), available at http://www.icj-cij.org/docket/files/143/16883.pdf.

law, JASTA does not limit litigation to cases where our government has determined that retaliation for terrorist support is justified. JASTA thus would undercut our ability to argue that the terrorism exception currently on the books constitutes a legitimate countermeasure permitted by international law.[3] Instead, it allows private parties to force a foreign sovereign into court, and thereby violates the international legal obligation to provide immunity from suit, upon the unsubstantiated claim of an aggrieved plaintiff. Such violations of existing international law encourage other states to do the same, thereby shrinking state immunity worldwide.

Many states, our allies as well as our adversaries, have questioned the legality of acts undertaken by the Bush and Obama administrations in response to terrorist threats. If this bill passes, private litigants will have greater reason to bring suits advancing those claims. Moreover, diplomatic efforts to shut down such litigation largely would be unavailing, because even sympathetic allies would not be able to interfere with private suits before independent courts. Nor would we be in a good position to ask our allies to enact laws increasing sovereign immunity to bar such suits, given the message that enactment of this bill would send. At the end of the day, increasing the exposure of our antiterrorism efforts to foreign legal liability does not seem like a sound way to combat terrorist threats.

Let me make this point concrete. In response to the judgment of the International Court of Justice, the Italian courts proved defiant. They struck down an act of their

---

[3] See Paul B. Stephan, Sovereign Immunity and the International Court of Justice: The State System Triumphant, in Foreign Affairs Litigation in United States Courts 67, 80-82 (John N. Moore ed., 2013).

parliament according immunity, declaring that the rights of persons to litigate their claims in Italian courts overrode core principles of international law.[4] Italy, you may recall, is also the country whose courts have brought criminal prosecutions against U.S. officials involved in apprehending suspected terrorists. These prosecutions arguably violate Italy's treaty commitments to us. Enactment of JASTA will encourage the Italian courts, already inclined to disregard general rules of international law as well as specific treaties, to create even more exceptions to sovereign immunity, just as JASTA does. This would expose the United States to severe civil litigation risk for counterterrorism activities. Other countries will notice and respond accordingly.

I mention Italy, an ally with whom we may have a few disagreements. What about our adversaries, countries where the governments often call the shots in their courts? Cuba and Iran already have taken away our immunity from suit as means of rallying domestic and international sympathy against us. If this bill passes, what countries will be next, citing this legislation as justification for their hostile acts?

Moreover, this bill will have direct and undesirable effects in our own court, not simply indirect effects on the policies of other states. Under this bill, those opposed to U.S. policy as carried out by our allies can bring suits that, I believe, this Congress would not want. To be specific, this bill opens the door not just for claims against states that might provide covert support for terrorism, but also against states that overtly used their police and military in what they consider self-defense, but others may characterize as

---

[4] Italian Constitutional Court, Judgment n. 238 of October 22nd, 2014 (unofficial English translation by Alessio Gracis, available at http://italyspractice.info/judgment-238-2014).

terrorism. We already have seen litigation in this country against Israeli officials and contractors for missile strikes and other measures taken against that country's adversaries.[5] Once this legislation passes, plaintiffs will be able sue Israel directly, asking our courts to adjudicate the line between self-defense and unlawful use of force.

Of course, Section 3(a)(2) of JASTA contains an exclusion from its rejection of immunity for acts of war, as defined by 18 U.S.C. § 2331(4). But in the hands of a good plaintiff's attorney, this exclusion serves as an invitation to litigate what counts as acts in the course of armed conflict, with the goal of labeling demolition of homes, police responses to riots and similar conduct as terrorism rather than armed conflict. To repeat myself, under this bill, it is enough to plead terrorism to haul a sovereign state into court, whatever the ultimate outcome of the trial.

Next, it is very unlikely that this bill will achieve its stated purpose. Most states, when confronted with lawsuits in foreign courts that they regard as violating their rights under international law, refuse to appear. When default judgments result, they refuse to pay them. Because this bill affects only amenability to suit, and does not deal with the broader immunity that foreign-state-owned assets enjoy from execution and attachment, it does not affect the incentives of foreign states to refuse to appear and to leave plaintiffs to the typically futile task of trying to track down attachable assets. As a result, the lawsuits that the bill would permit are unlikely to unearth evidence that would identify,

---

[5] E.g., Matar v. Dichter, 563 F.3d 9 (2d Cir. 2009) (suit against head of Shin Bet for missile strikes against Palestinian targets); Corrie v. Caterpillar, Inc., 503 F.3d 974 (9th Cir. 2007) (suit against American contractor for supplying bulldozers used to demolish buildings in Occupied Territories).

much less punish, state sponsors of terrorism or to produce acknowledgments of culpability accompanied by compensation.

This Committee would do well to heed the words of Judge Royce Lamberth, who has logged more time handling cases under the current terrorism exception to the Foreign Sovereign Immunities Act than any other judge:

Today, the Court also reaches an even more fundamental conclusion: Civil litigation against Iran under the FSIA state sponsor of terrorism exception represents a failed policy. After more than a decade spent presiding over these difficult cases, this Court now sees that these cases do not achieve justice for victims, are not sustainable, and threaten to undermine the President's foreign policy initiatives during a particularly critical time in our Nation's history. The truth is that the prospects for recovery upon judgments entered in these cases are extremely remote. The amount of Iranian assets currently known to exist with the United States is approximately 45 million dollars, which is infinitesimal in comparison to the 10 billion dollars in currently outstanding court judgments. Beyond the lack of assets available for execution of judgments, however, these civil actions inevitably must confront deeply entrenched and fundamental understandings of foreign state sovereignty, conflicting multinational treaties and executive agreements, and the exercise of presidential executive power in an ever-changing and increasingly complex world of international affairs.[6]

---

[6] In re Islamic Republic of Iran Terrorism Litigation, 659 F. Supp. 2d 31, 37 (D.D.C. 2009).

I can update Judge Lamberth's remarks by pointing out that the most recent effort by Congress to enforce payment of the Iranian terror judgments, a provision of the Iran Threat Reduction and Syria Human Rights Act of 2012 codified at 22 U.S.C. § 8772, has led to a lawsuit filed by Iran against the United States in the International Court of Justice.[7] We must contemplate the unpleasant possibility that any money collected under Section 8772 ultimately will be paid by the United States.

I appreciate that the intended target of JASTA is Saudi Arabia, and I have no knowledge as to whether that state has attachable assets in the United States. This bill, however, is not limited to that country. If Congress wants to pursue that particular state, so be it. But JASTA ranges much more widely, and creates much more mischief to little apparent benefit.

Finally, there is something seriously wrong with privatizing American national security policy. State support of terrorism has consumed the Executive and Congress for many decades, going back at least to the 1970s. Significant legislative tools exist to punish states, including the imposition of severe sanctions. The lynchpin of all these efforts is that the Executive and Congress together determine which states sponsor terrorism. Once they make this determination, U.S. courts are open to claims for compensation.[8]

---

[7] "Iran institutes proceedings against the United States with regard to a dispute concerning alleged violations of the 1955 Treaty of Amity," Press Release of the International Court of Justice, June 15, 2016, available at http://www.icj-cij.org/docket/files/164/19032.pdf.

[8] 28 U.S.C. § 1605A(a)(1) (no immunity for claims based, among other things, on "provision of material support or resources" for specified acts of terrorism).

This bill, if enacted, would not alter the substantive rules imposing civil liability for state sponsorship of terrorism. Our law already provides right to compensation for victims of state-sponsored terrorism. What this bill does is allow a private litigant to leapfrog the political branches simply by alleging that a particular state sponsors terrorism, based on belief and hope rather than proof. It leaves the decision of when to discard sovereign immunity, with all the risks that this step entails, to private litigants acting on incomplete information and whose interests that do not necessarily match those of our nation as a whole. Under this bill, once a suit begins, the Executive loses control over the process. Although Section 5 of JASTA allows the judge to stay the suit, the bill still leaves it to the court and the litigants to decide whether to do so. If they regard the efforts of the Executive to unearth evidence of state support for terrorism as unsatisfactory, this bill gives them a green light to go forward.

State support of terrorism is a grave act, justifying in response strong economic sanctions and, in appropriate circumstances, armed force, as the United States undertook in Libya in 1986. Outsourcing to private litigants the profound determination of whether a foreign state has supported an attack on us simply makes no sense. The purpose of private litigation is mostly to get compensation, which is to say to get paid. Its job is not to decide as a matter of first instance whether grave assaults on U.S. security have occurred. We have an extensive national security establishment, including the intelligence and defense communities, to find these things out. Expecting private litigants to perform these vital tasks disrupts rather than furthers our antiterrorism efforts.

In sum, this bill, if enacted, would harm U.S. interests by putting the United States in violation of international law and eroding the protection that we now enjoy from hostile litigation overseas, would not advance the cause of identifying state supporters of terrorism, and likely would interfere with our current antiterrorism activities. It should be rejected.

———

Mr. FRANKS. I thank the gentleman, and now recognize our fourth and final witness, Mr. Gurulé. Sir, if you would turn that microphone on, too.

TESTIMONY OF JIMMY GURULÉ, PROFESSOR OF LAW, NOTRE DAME LAW SCHOOL

Mr. GURULÉ . Chairman Franks, Ranking Member Cohen, and other distinguished Members of the Subcommittee, I would like to thank you for holding this important hearing on the Justice Against Sponsors of Terrorism Act, and inviting me to testify on the value of this legislation in combating the threat of global terrorism.

As we approach the 15 year anniversary of the 9/11 terrorist attacks that tragically took the lives of approximately 3,000 innocent civilians, it is imperative that the U.S. Government continue to strengthen the effectiveness of its counterterrorism efforts, including depriving terrorists of funding, as well as deterring and punishing their financial sponsors, including foreign states.

The enactment of JASTA is critical to achieving that objective. I would like to just briefly comment on three points—the first is the important goals advanced by JASTA; second, the fact that JASTA is narrowly drafted, narrowly tailored; and third, debunking the reciprocity arguments that are clearly, in my opinion, overstated. First, on the goals of JASTA—civil tort actions that seek large monetary damages provide an invaluable supplement to the criminal justice process and administrative blocking orders.

These civil tort actions—claims, excuse me—advance five important goals—first, private lawsuits brought by victims of terrorism can have a deterrent effect against foreign governments that support acts of terrorism. While the threat of large civil monetary judgment may have little or no deterrent effect against the terrorists themselves, the same may not be true for foreign governments that lend financial support and direction to foreign terrorist organizations.

These foreign states are likely to have substantial assets in the United State that may be attached to enforce civil terrorism judgments. We have seen that recently with the Islamic Republic of Iran, that recently has been sued by the victims of the 1983 terror attacks in Beirut, and their assets in the United States, approximately $1.7 billion in assets in the United States, have been attached to enforce the terrorism judgement against Iran.

No one can tell me that that type of action, seizing those types of assets against a foreign state, is not going to have any deterrent effect against that foreign state with respect to its future activities, with respect to supporting acts of terrorism.

Second, civil actions targeting the assets of foreign states that support terrorism can reduce the ability of international terrorists to carry out their deadly attacks. Money is the life blood of terrorists. While terrorists seldom kill for money, they always need money to kill. Depriving terrorists of funding, especially from foreign state sponsors of terrorism, is critical to preventing terrorist attacks and saving innocent lives.

Third, foreign states that sponsor terrorism, including through government charities, should be held accountable for their action. That is a very fundamental principal and proposition.

Fourth, victims of international terrorism should be compensated for their unimaginable loss, pain and suffering. And the foreign states responsible for these physical and emotional injuries should be held responsible for that compensation.

And finally, the JASTA strengthens the statutory framework of the Foreign Sovereign Immunities Act and the Antiterrorism Act, and confirms the importance of civil litigation as an important tool in combating terrorism. With respect to JASTA itself, it is a very narrowly-tailored statute, and applies extremely limited and extraordinary circumstances, and does not permit U.S. nationals to routinely sue foreign states, as some critics of the legislation have maintained.

First, it has a geographic limitation; it only applies to acts of terrorism that occur in the United States. As a subject matter limitation, it only applies to acts of international terrorism, not other acts of violence; and international terrorism is a well-defined term in the Federal U.S. Statute 18 U.S.C. 2331.

Fourth, the term international terrorism excludes any act of war, so that would not be covered in this legislation; it would not justify the cause of action for such actions. It is limited to actions that are aided and abetted by foreign terrorist organizations—that is another limitation. There is approximate cause limitation on the statutes, so these would be acts of international terrorism that were caused by the foreign state that aided and abetted the terrorist organization.

Further, the statute provides that it does not extend to negligent acts—negligence by the foreign state—but only intentional or knowing conduct involving the state.

And with respect to aiding and abetting, the statute provides that the foreign state must have provided substantial assistance to the foreign terrorist organization.

With respect to the last point, on the overstatement regarding the reciprocity concerns, let me just simply say countries with the greatest potential for such lawsuits against the United States have authoritarian regimes that do not permit their citizens to bring civil suits against foreign governments for acts of international terrorism. In those countries, such actions are the exclusive purgative of the authoritarian government.

For example, the private civil terrorism lawsuit filed against Iran for its complicity in the 1983 terrorist attack in Beirut, Lebanon, killing over 200 American servicemen, did not result in retaliatory lawsuits be filed against the United States by private citizens in Iran.

Furthermore, the civil terrorism case did not undermine the U.S. Government's efforts to finalize the joint comprehensive plan of action with the Islamic Republic of Iran. The civil terrorism lawsuit was pending when the United States and its allies were negotiating and finalizing the terms of the multilateral agreement with Iran to limit the country's ability to develop nuclear weapons.

So it had no effect—the fact is the pending terrorism suit had no effect on that. So I think that the statement regarding retaliation is largely overstated.

And finally, in conclusion, the JASTA eliminates sovereign immunity for foreign states that intentionally, knowingly, aid and abet terrorist organizations in carrying out deadly attacks on U.S. soil; in my opinion that is good U.S. policy, and as a result, the JASTA should be enacted into law by Congress. Thank you.

[The prepared statement of Mr. Gurulé follows:]

UNIVERSITY OF
NOTRE DAME
THE LAW SCHOOL

Written Testimony of

Jimmy Gurulé
Professor of Law
Notre Dame Law School

Hearing Before the House Judiciary Committee
Subcommittee on the Constitution and Civil Justice
Washington, D.C.

July 14, 2016

Written Testimony of
Jimmy Gurulé
Professor of Law
Notre Dame Law School

Hearing Before the House Judiciary Committee,
Subcommittee on the Constitution and Civil Justice
July 14, 2016

Chairman Franks, Ranking Member Cohen, and other distinguished members of the House Judiciary Committee, Subcommittee on the Constitution and Civil Justice:

I would like to thank you for holding this important hearing on the Justice Against Sponsors of Terrorism Act (JASTA) and inviting me to testify on the value of this legislation in combating the threat of global terrorism.

As we approach the fifteen-year anniversary of the 9/11 terrorist attacks that tragically took the lives of approximately 3,000 innocent civilians, it is imperative that the U.S. government continue to strengthen the effectiveness of its counter-terrorism efforts, including depriving terrorists of funding, as well as deterring and punishing their financial sponsors. The enactment of the JASTA is critical to achieving that objective.

(A) Statutory Overview

On May 17, 2016, the U.S. Senate unanimously passed the JASTA in an effort to enhance civil terrorism causes of action and deter acts of terrorism.[1] This legislation ensures that those who aid and abet terrorist attacks on U.S. soil are held accountable for their conduct, even if such offenders are foreign sovereigns or their agencies or instrumentalities. The JASTA does so through modest amendments to the Foreign Sovereign Immunities Act (FSIA)[2] and the Anti-Terrorism Act (ATA).[3] The JASTA is a narrowly drawn statute that will deter international terrorism, guarantee the victims of terrorist attacks their day in court, and grant the executive new powers to resolve civil terrorism cases through diplomatic means. More specifically, the JASTA ensures that U.S. courts will have jurisdiction over cases involving injury or death of U.S. nationals caused by an act international terrorism on U.S. soil that is committed or substantially aided and abetted by a foreign state.

The bill's new sovereign immunity exception amends chapter 97 of Title 28 of the U.S. Code by inserting § 1605B, which provides in relevant part:

---

[1] Justice Against Sponsors of Terrorism Act, S. 2040, 114th Cong., § 3(a) (as passed by Senate, May 17, 2016). [hereinafter "JASTA"].

[2] 28 U.S.C. §§ 1602-1611 (1976). Section 1604 provides:

> Subject to existing international agreements to which the United States is a party at the time of enactment of this Act a foreign state shall be immune from the jurisdiction of the courts of the United States and of the States except as provided in sections 1605 to 1607 of this chapter.

[3] 18 U.S.C. § 2333 is the civil remedies provision of the ATA, added Oct. 29, 1992, Pub. L. No. 102-572, Title X, § 1003(a)(4), 106 Stat. 4506, codified as amended.

> A foreign state shall not be immune from the jurisdiction of the courts of the United States in any case in which money damages are sought against a foreign state for physical injury to person or property or death occurring in the United States and caused by (1) an act of international terrorism in the United States; and (2) a tortious act or acts of the foreign state, or of any official, employee, or ... agency, regardless where the tortious act or acts of the foreign state occurred.[4]

Under the JASTA, foreign states that knowingly aid and abet foreign terrorist organizations (FTOs) that commit terrorist attacks in the United States which kill or seriously injure Americans will be held accountable for their conduct.

The JASTA provides that, where the jurisdictional criteria against a foreign state are satisfied, a U.S. national may bring a tort claim against that foreign state pursuant to the ATA. The ATA, 18 U.S.C. § 2333, created a private right of action for any U.S. national injured or killed by reason of an act of international terrorism. Federal courts are currently divided on whether § 2333 allows claims based on a theory of aiding and abetting an act of international terrorism.[5] Disagreement on the scope of the ATA is untenable and could lead to inconsistent verdicts across circuits depending on whether a plaintiff must prove that the defendant committed the act of international terrorism, or merely aided and abetted some other actor in doing so. The JASTA eliminates this confusion by expressly recognizing a cause of action against a foreign state for aiding and abetting an FTO in the very narrow circumstance of committing international terrorism on U.S. soil.[6]

Sponsors of the JASTA recognize that terror victims' demands for justice may complicate international diplomacy in certain circumstances. To address this concern, § 5 of the JASTA gives the President the power to intervene in any civil litigation against a foreign state alleging support for international terrorism, and obtain a stay of the proceedings while government-to-government discussions proceed between the United States and that foreign state. Ultimately, the JASTA will allow families victimized by terrorism to proceed in court against the terrorists and their sponsors, and hold them accountable for their actions. For all of the above reasons, this proposed legislation is critical to preventing terrorist attacks and saving innocent lives, and should be enacted into law.

(B) Important Goals Advanced by the JASTA

"[C]ivil tort actions that seek large monetary damages provide an invaluable supplement to the criminal justice process and administrative blocking orders."[7] These civil terrorism tort claims advance five important goals. First, private lawsuits brought by the victims of terrorism

---

[4] JASTA, § 3(a).

[5] *See* Jimmy Gurulé, *Holding Banks Liable Under the Anti-Terrorism Act for Providing Financial Services to Terrorists: An Ineffective Remedy in Need of Reform*, 41 N.D. J. Leg. 184, 206-09 (2015) [hereinafter "*Holding Banks Liable Under the Anti-Terrorism Act*"].

[6] *See* JASTA, § 4. Section 4 also authorizes tort liability for conspiring to commit an act of international terrorism.

[7] Jimmy Gurulé, UNFUNDING TERROR: THE LEGAL RESPONSE TO THE FINANCING OF GLOBAL TERRORISM, at 324 (2008) (discussing the important role of civil suits in bankrupting terrorist organizations); *see also* Halberstam v. Welch, 705 F.2d 472, 489 (D.C. Cir. 1983)

78

can have a deterrent effect against donors, corrupt charities, financial institutions, and foreign governments that provide funding and logistical support to terrorist organizations.[8] While the threat of large civil monetary judgments may have little or no deterrent effect against the terrorists themselves, the same may not be true for foreign governments that lend financial support and direction to FTOs. These foreign states are likely to have substantial assets in the United States that may be attached to enforce a civil terrorism judgment. Furthermore, civil terrorism judgments can be extremely large, totaling hundreds of millions or even billions of dollars in damages.[9] As such, the threat of large civil terrorism judgments can have a deterrent effect and influence the behavior of terrorist sympathizers.

Second, civil actions targeting the assets of foreign states that support terrorism can reduce the ability of international terrorists to carry out their deadly attacks.[10] Money is the "lifeblood" of terrorists.[11] While "[t]errorists seldom kill for money . . . they always need money to kill."[12] Depriving terrorists of funding, especially from foreign state supporters of terrorism, is critical to preventing terrorist attacks and saving innocent lives.

Third, foreign states that sponsor terrorism, including through government "charities," should be held accountable for their actions. Foreign states should not be permitted to conduct business in the United States and use the profits generated from their commercial ventures to support acts of terrorism. Depriving state sponsors of terrorism of their assets located in the United States punishes them for their unlawful conduct. The JASTA conveys an important message to foreign states that might support terrorism or allow their employees or institutions to do so: If you support acts of terrorism, you run the risk of being sued, held liable for your unlawful conduct, and having your assets attached to enforce a civil terrorism judgment. Furthermore, the financial losses in these lawsuits can be substantial.

Fourth, victims of international terrorism should be compensated for their unimaginable loss, pain, and suffering, and the foreign states responsible for these physical and emotional injuries should be responsible for such compensation.

Finally, the JASTA strengthens the statutory framework of the FSIA and ATA and confirms the importance of civil litigation as an important took in combating terrorism. The FSIA,

___

[8] *Id.*; *see also* Antiterrorism Act of 1990: Hearing Before the Subcomm. on Courts and Administrative Practice of Comm. on the Judiciary, 101st Cong., 2d Sess. 79 (1990) ("[A]nything that could be done to deter . . . money laundering in the United States, the repose of assets in the United States . . . would not only help benefit victims, but would also help deter terrorism.").

[9] *See, e.g.*, Bank Markazi v. Peterson, No. 14-770, Slip Op. (Apr. 20, 2016) (authorizing the attachment of approximately $1.7 billion in assets belonging to Bank Markazi, the Central Bank of Iran, to enforce terrorism judgments against Iran for aiding and abetting several attacks, including the 1983 terrorist bombing of the Marine barracks in Beirut, Lebanon that killed over 200 American servicemen).

[10] UNFUNDING TERROR, note 7 at 325.

[11] *See* NATIONAL COMMISSION ON TERRORIST ATTACKS, THE 9/11 COMMISSION REPORT, FINAL REPORT OF THE NATIONAL COMMISSION ON TERRORIST ATTACKS UPON THE UNITED STATES 382 (W.W. Norton & Company 2004), http://www.9-11commission.gov/report/911Report.pdf ("The government has recognized that information about terrorist money helps us to understand their networks, search them out, and disrupt their operations.").

[12] Terry Davis, Secretary General of the Council of Europe, Plenary of MONEYVAL and Financial Action Task Force, Feb. 21, 2007.

28 U.S.C. § 1605A, waives the sovereign immunity of foreign states and their agents by creating a "terrorism exception" for injury or death caused by acts of "torture, extrajudicial killing, aircraft sabotage, hostage taking, or the provision of material support or resources."[13] The terrorism exception only waives the immunity of a foreign state "designated as a state sponsor of terrorism at the time the [terrorist] act . . . occurred, or was so designated as a result of such act."[14] There are currently three states that have been designated by the Secretary of State as state sponsors of terrorism: Iran, Sudan, and Syria.[15] Other states, such as Saudi Arabia[16] and North Korea, retain foreign sovereign immunity from litigation under the FSIA.

In civil actions brought under § 1605A of the FSIA, plaintiffs are entitled to "economic damages, solatium, pain and suffering, and punitive damages."[17] Furthermore, under the FSIA, a "foreign state shall be liable in the same manner and to the same extent as a private individual under like circumstances."[18]

The ATA, 18 U.S.C. § 2333, authorizes a civil cause of action for U.S. nationals victimized by acts of international terrorism against terrorists and their supporters. In enacting the ATA, Congress intended to deter and punish acts of international terrorism by "remov[ing] the jurisdictional hurdles . . . and . . . empower[ing] victims with all the weapons available in civil litigation."[19] However, the ATA does not authorize suits against foreign states.

The JASTA fills an important gap in the law by permitting U.S. nationals to bring suit against foreign states, even those states not formally designated by the State Department as an FTO, that aid and abet terrorists that commit acts of international terrorism in the United States and kill and injure Americans. The enactment of the FSIA terrorism exception and the ATA demonstrates the vital importance of civil actions in deterring and punishing acts of international terrorism.[20] The JASTA is further recognition of the value of civil actions to combat the threat of terrorism.[21]

---

[13] 28 U.S.C. § 1605A(a)(2).

[14] *Id.*

[15] *See* U.S. Dep't of State, State Sponsors of Terrorism, www.state.gov/j/ct/list/c14151.html (last visited July 7, 2016).

[16] *See* In re Terrorist Attacks on Sept. 11, 2001, 538 F.3d 71, 89 (2d Cir. 2008) ("The State Department has never designated the Kingdom a state sponsor of terrorism. As a consequence, the Terrorism Exception is inapplicable here.").

[17] 28 U.S.C. § 1605A.

[18] *Id.* § 1606.

[19] 137 Cong. Rec. S4511-04, S4511 (1991) (statement of Sen. Grassley). The Alien Tort Claims Act, 28 U.S.C. § 1350, has also been used to hold defendants civilly liable for acts of international terrorism. *See, e.g.,* Almog v. Arab Bank, PLC, 471 F. Supp. 2d 257, 279 (E.D.N.Y. 2007) (holding that terrorist bombing is a violation of the law of nations).

[20] *See* Estates of Ungar ex rel. Strachman v. Palestinian Authority, 304 F. Supp. 2d 232, 238-39 (D.R.I. 2004); *see also* 136 Cong. Rec. S4568-01, S4593 (1990) (statement of Sen Grassley) ("With the enactment of this legislation [the ATA], we set an example to the world of how the United States legal system deals with terrorists. If terrorists have assets within our jurisdictional reach, American citizens will have the power to seize them.").

[21] *See* JASTA, § X Findings and Purpose:

The United States has a vital interest in providing persons and entities injured as a result of terrorist attacks committed within the United States with the full access to the court system in order to

(C) JASTA is Narrowly Tailored

The JASTA removes foreign sovereign immunity and authorizes a civil cause of action in extremely limited and extraordinary circumstances. The proposed legislation does not permit U.S. nationals to routinely sue foreign states as some critics of the legislation maintain.[22] The JASTA imposes a geographic limitation on civil terrorism actions. Section 3 eliminates sovereign immunity for injury or death caused by an act of international terrorism occurring in the United States.[23] The JASTA does not confer jurisdiction on U.S. courts if the foreign state sponsored a terrorist attack that killed or seriously injured U.S. nationals abroad.

The JASTA permits jurisdiction for injury or death caused by an act of "international terrorism."[24] The term "international terrorism" has the same meaning given the term in 18 U.S.C. § 2331, which requires proof of three essential elements. First, the conduct condemned must involve "violent acts" or "acts dangerous to human life" that are a violation of the criminal laws of the United States or any State.[25] Violations of the federal material support statutes, 18 U.S.C. § 2339A, § 2339B, and the terrorism financing statute, 18 U.S.C. § 2339C, have been construed by the courts to involve "acts dangerous to human life" for purposes of § 2331, and therefore constitute acts of "international terrorism" within the meaning of the ATA.[26]

Second, the definition of "international terrorism" requires that the prohibited conduct "appear to be intended" to intimidate or coerce a civilian population"; "influence the policy of a government by intimidation or coercion"; or "affect the conduct of a government by mass destruction, assassination, or kidnapping."[27] This "appear to be intended" language does not impose a state of mind requirement on the defendant. Instead, whether the subject conduct appears to be intended for any of those prohibited purposes "is a matter of external appearances rather than subjective intent."[28]

Third, § 2331's definition of "international terrorism" requires proof that the prohibited conduct has an extraterritorial nexus. Plaintiffs must prove that the terrorist-related acts occurred "primarily outside the territorial jurisdiction of the United States" or "transcend national boundaries."[29] Under the statute, plaintiffs can satisfy this extraterritorial requirement in three ways: "(1) the terrorist acts were accomplished by transcending national boundaries, (2) the persons the terrorist acts were intended to intimidate or coerce transcended national boundaries, or

---

pursue civil claims against persons, entities, or countries that have knowingly or recklessly provided material support or resources, directly or indirectly, to the persons or organizations responsible for their injuries.

[22] *See* Sean P. Carter, Jack Quinn & James P. Kreindler, *Saudi Arabia and 9/11: Give the American People the Truth, Mr. Obama*, FOX NEWS (Apr. 20, 2016), http://www.foxnews.com/opinion/2016/04/20/saudi-arabia-and-911-american-people-truth-mr-obama.print.html.

[23] *See* JASTA, § 3.

[24] *Id.*

[25] 18 U.S.C. § 2331(1)(A).

[26] 18 U.S.C. § 2333(a). *See also Holding Banks Liable Under the Anti-Terrorism Act*, *supra* note 5, at 190 n.41.

[27] 18 U.S.C. § 2331(B)(i)-(iii).

[28] Boim v. Holy Land Found. for Relief and Dev., 549 F.3d 685, 694 (7th Cir. 2008) (en banc).

[29] 18 U.S.C. § 2331(1)(C).

(3) the terrorist perpetrators conducted their operations abroad or after perpetrating their attack, they sought asylum or a safe haven in a foreign country."[30] Therefore, the JASTA does not lift sovereign immunity for all violent acts committed by foreign terrorists on U.S. soil, but only those acts that also have an extraterritorial nexus as defined by 18 U.S.C. § 2331.

The term "international terrorism" is further defined in the JASTA to exclude any "act of war" as defined in § 2331.[31] The JASTA thus affirms the critical distinction between legitimate military actions and acts of international terrorism, and therefore does not eliminate sovereign immunity for alleged war crimes committed against the United States during an armed conflict.

Additionally, for purposes of JASTA's substantive cause of action, the terrorist attack must have been committed, planned, or authorized by an organization that has been designated as a "foreign terrorist organization" or "FTO" under § 219 of the Immigration and Nationality Act.[32] This limitation further confirms that the JASTA is focused on defending our national security against the most notorious terrorist organizations.

The JASTA imposes another important limitation on civil liability. The death or injury must have been "caused by" an act of international terrorism.[33] To be found liable under the JASTA, the foreign state must have been the proximate cause of the plaintiffs' injuries. The civil proximate cause standard has two central components. First, the defendant's conduct must have been a "substantial factor" in the resultant harm.[34] Second, the injury must have been "reasonably foreseeable" as a natural consequence of the defendant's conduct.[35] As such, a foreign state that provides material support to an FTO is not strictly liable for every act of international terrorism committed by that FTO. To prevail, plaintiffs must prove that the financial assistance or other support provided by the foreign state to the terrorist organization was a "substantial factor" in causing the plaintiffs' losses and injuries, and that it was "reasonably foreseeable" that the provision of such support would cause the resultant harm.[36]

Furthermore, the JASTA does not waive sovereign immunity of a foreign state for "an omission or a tortious act or acts that constitute mere negligence."[37] A foreign state must intentionally, knowingly, or recklessly aid and abet the FTO responsible for causing serious injury or death to U.S. nationals on U.S. soil. Liability cannot be based on mere negligent conduct.

---

[30] Jimmy Gurulé & Geoffrey Corn, PRINCIPLES OF COUNTER-TERRORISM LAW, at 373 (2010); see also 18 U.S.C. § 2331(1)(C).

[31] See JASTA, § 3.

[32] 8 U.S.C. § 1189. Under § 1189(a)(1)(A)-(C), the Secretary of State, in consultation with the Secretary of the Treasury and Attorney General, may designate a foreign organization as a "foreign terrorist organization" upon finding that "(1) the organization is a foreign organization, (2) the organization engages in terrorist activity or retains the capability and intent to engage in terrorist activity, and (3) the terrorist activity threatens the national security or the security of United States nationals."

[33] See JASTA, § 3.

[34] See Holding Banks Liable Under the Anti-Terrorism Act, supra note 5, at 203.

[35] Id.

[36] Id.

[37] JASTA, § 3.

Therefore, a foreign state that was merely negligent in supervising its officials, employees, or agents that provided such assistance to an FTO could not be sued under the JASTA.

Finally, if plaintiffs are proceeding under a theory of aiding and abetting, they must prove that the foreign state provided "substantial assistance" to the FTO responsible for the terrorist attack.[38] The "Findings and Purpose" section of the JASTA makes clear that aiding and abetting liability should be governed by the seminal case of *Halberstam v. Welch*, 705 F.2d 472 (D.C. Cir. 1983), which defines and elaborates on the meaning of "substantial assistance." Proof of "substantial assistance" requires "more than just a little aid."[39] At a minimum, it requires "knowledge of the illegal activity that is being aided and abetted, a desire to help that activity succeed, and some act to further such activity to make it succeed."[40]

In sum, the JASTA is a narrowly-tailored and carefully-crafted statute, creating a cause of action for a limited category of claims where plaintiffs have suffered injury or loss of loved ones by reason of an act of international terrorism committed within the United States by a designated FTO. Further, the JASTA removes sovereign immunity and seeks to hold accountable a narrow category of foreign states that intentionally, knowingly, or recklessly provide substantial assistance to an FTO, where the plaintiffs' injuries or losses were a reasonably foreseeable consequence of the foreign state's assistance and such assistance was a substantial factor in causing the resultant harm.

(D) Debunking the Reciprocity Argument

The Obama Administration opposes the JASTA, claiming that it violates principles of sovereign immunity and will cause harmful, reciprocal effects abroad.[41] According to President Obama, "[if] we open up the possibility that individuals in the United States can routinely start suing other governments, then we are also opening up the United States to being sued by individuals in other countries."[42] However, sovereign immunity is not absolute, and does not exempt governments from suits in foreign countries. In fact, governments have long been subject to civil suits in foreign countries for their wrongful acts. Furthermore, as previously discussed, the JASTA is a narrowly-tailored statute and does not permit U.S. citizens to "routinely" sue foreign states, which substantially minimizes the possibility of retaliatory lawsuits.

The immunity of foreign states is governed by the FSIA, which grants foreign states as well as their agencies and instrumentalities immunity from suit in the United States subject to several enumerated exceptions.[43] Under the FSIA, a foreign state is presumptively immune from

---

[38] *See* JASTA, § 4.

[39] Goldberg v. UBS AG, 660 F. Supp. 2d 410, 429 (E.D.N.Y. 2009) (quoting Barker v. Henderson, Franklin, Starnes & Holt, 797 F.2d 490 (7th Cir. 1986)).

[40] *Goldberg*, 660 F. Supp. 2d at 425 (quoting United States v. Zafiro, 945 F.2d 881, 887 (7th Cir. 1991), *aff'd*, 506 U.S. 534 (1993)).

[41] *See Saudi Arabia and 9/11, supra* note 22 (White House Press Secretary Josh Earnest claims that the JASTA threatens "the whole notion of sovereign immunity").

[42] *Id.*

[43] *See* FSIA, *supra* note 2, at § 1604.

the jurisdiction of U.S. courts and federal courts lack subject-matter jurisdiction over a claim against a foreign state unless a statutory exception applies.

Section 1605(a)(5), the torts exception of the FSIA creates such an exception, and subjects foreign governments to suit in U.S. courts for tortious acts of foreign governments and their agents that cause harm in the United States.[44] Section 1605(a)(5) provides that a foreign state shall not be immune from the jurisdiction of the courts of the United States in any case --

> [I]n which money damages are sought against a foreign state for personal injury or death, or damage to or loss of property, occurring in the United States and caused by the tortious act or omission of that foreign state or of any official or employee of that foreign state while acting within the scope of his office or employment.[45]

Thus, U.S. laws already subject foreign states to suit in our courts when they cause injury domestically. However, the fact that foreign governments can be sued in the United States has not triggered retaliatory lawsuits that imperil the interests of the United States or its citizens abroad.

The International Court of Justice has examined international practice in this area and concluded that the international norm for sovereign immunity is that a "State is not entitled to immunity in respect of torts occasioning death, personal injury or damage to property occurring on the territory of the [enacting] State."[46] Thus, the U.S. government is already subject to suit abroad when its conduct causes such an injury in a foreign country.

More fundamentally, the risk of foreign lawsuits has existed for forty years. Since its enactment in 1976, the FSIA has contained a broad exception to immunity for tort claims, which includes actions for wrongful death and other serious injuries caused by international terrorism.[47] Only recently have courts exempted acts of terrorism from the FSIA tort exception.[48] However, despite the existence of the FSIA tort exception there has not been a flood of foreign lawsuits filed against the United States.

Countries with the greatest potential for such lawsuits against the United States have authoritarian regimes that do not permit their citizens to bring civil suits against foreign governments for acts of international terrorism. In those countries, such actions are the exclusive prerogative of the authoritarian government. For example, the private civil terrorism lawsuit filed against Iran for its complicity in the 1983 terrorist attack in Beirut, Lebanon, killing over 200

---

[44] *See* FSIA, *supra* note 2, at § 1605(a)(5).

[45] *Id.* Section 1605(a)(5)(A) provides an exception to the tort exception: "[Section (a)(5) shall not apply to] any claim based upon the exercise or performance or the failure to exercise or perform a discretionary function regardless of whether the discretion be abused."

[46] Jurisdictional Immunities of the State (Germany v. Italy: Greece Intervening) Judgment, ICJ Reports 2012, 99, http://www.icj-cij.org/docket/files/143/16883.pdf.

[47] *See* Liu v. Republic of China, 892 F.2d 1419, 1424-25 (9th Cir. 1989) (holding that the FSIA tort exception provides jurisdiction over Taiwan for claims alleging its agents' complicity in an act of extrajudicial killing on U.S. soil); Letelier v. Republic of Chile, 488 F. Supp. 665, 671 (D.D.C. 1980) (holding that the FSIA tort exception provides for jurisdiction over Chile for the extrajudicial killing by one of its agents in the United States).

[48] *See e.g.*, Burnett v. Al Baraka Inv. & Dev. Corp., 292 F. Supp. 2d 9, 17-21 (D.D.C. 2003); In re Terrorist Attacks on Sept. 11, 2001, 349 F. Supp. 2d 765 (S.D.N.Y. 2005).

American servicemen, did not result in retaliatory lawsuits being filed against the United States by private citizens in Iran.[49] Furthermore, the civil terrorism case did not undermine the U.S. government's efforts to finalize the Joint Comprehensive Plan of Action with the Islamic Republic of Iran. The civil terrorism lawsuit was pending when the United States and its allies were negotiating and finalizing the terms of the multi-lateral agreement with Iran to limit that country's ability to develop nuclear weapons.

Despite suggestion by some Administration officials to the contrary, the JASTA would not subject U.S. diplomats to suit in foreign countries. Diplomatic immunity is governed by the Vienna Convention on Diplomatic Relations, to which the United States and 189 countries are signatories.[50] The JASTA does not alter the immunity of diplomats under that Convention. Furthermore, the JASTA has no effect on foreign suits filed against private U.S. citizens abroad. If a U.S. citizen commits a wrongful act that injures someone in a foreign country, that country's domestic laws would determine whether the U.S. citizen could be subject to suit.

The FSIA tort exception could be read to provide jurisdiction in U.S. courts for claims relating to acts of international terrorism on U.S. soil. However, federal courts are currently divided on the issue. Some courts have interpreted the FSIA tort exception as providing for jurisdiction to address acts of terrorism and extrajudicial killings on U.S. soil.[51] Other courts have denied such terrorism-related claims based on the tort exception.[52] Among other things, the JASTA resolves this conflict, expressly removing sovereign immunity for foreign states that sponsor acts of international terrorism occurring in the United States. The JASTA largely reaffirms the fundamental understanding of U.S. sovereign immunity law, in particular, that foreign states will not be immune for torts causing injury on U.S. soil, including wrongful death and other injuries resulting from acts of international terrorism.

The JASTA is a narrowly drafted statute that removes sovereign immunity in only extraordinary circumstances. Because of the limited scope of application of the JASTA, the fear that U.S. nationals will routinely file suits against foreign governments for acts of international terrorism, resulting in retaliatory lawsuits being filed against the United States is baseless.

(E) Conclusion

The emergence of the Islamic State and the resurgence of al Qaeda present grave threats to our national security. Curtailing the funding of these terrorist organizations is critical to preventing terrorist attacks on the homeland and the deaths of innocent civilians. The risk of being sued under the JASTA and having hundreds of millions of dollars of assets attached to enforce a civil terrorism judgment serves as a powerful deterrent to reckless foreign governments. Civil terrorism lawsuits could cause such foreign governments to stop providing financial support and assistance to FTOs intent on killing Americans, thereby depriving terrorists of funding. The legislation would also

---

[49] *See Bank Markazi v. Peterson*, No. 14-770 (U.S.S.C. 2016),

[50] *See* Vienna Convention on Diplomatic Relations, Apr. 18, 1961, 23 U.S.T. 3227, T.I.A.S. No. 7502, http://untreaty.un.org/ilc/texts/instruments/english/conventions/9_1_1961.pdf.

[51] *See, e.g., Liu*, 892 F.2d at 1419; *Letelier*, 488 F. Supp. at 665.

[52] *See, e.g., Burnett*, 292 F. Supp. 2d at 17-21; *In re Terrorist Attacks on Sept. 11, 2001*, 349 F. Supp. 2d at 765.

provide an incentive for foreign states to adequately regulate and police governmental-religious institutions and charities.

The JASTA eliminates sovereign immunity for foreign states that intentionally, knowingly or recklessly aid and abet terrorist organizations in carrying out deadly attacks on U.S. soil. That is good policy. The JASTA should therefore be enacted into law by Congress.

Thank you for the opportunity to appear before the Subcommittee on the Constitution and Civil Justice on this important topic. At this time, I would be pleased to answer any questions.

––––––––––

Mr. FRANKS. And I thank you all for your testimony, and we will now proceed under the 5 minute rule of questions, and I will begin by recognizing myself for 5 minutes. And, Judge Mukasey, I will start with you sir. First, thank you for your gallant service to the country.

Mr. MUKASEY. Thank you very much.

Mr. FRANKS. Judge Mukasey, JASTA essentially calls on Congress to strike a balance between providing U.S. victims of terrorism with access to judicial redress for terrorist attacks on U.S. soil that our sponsored by foreign governments, and subjecting foreign governments to lawsuits is U.S. courts—at least that is the attempt, I think, of the legislation.

Why do you think JASTA strikes this balance incorrectly? Can you help us understand that?

Mr. MUKASEY. I think the principal problem with that analysis is that JASTA does not itself determine its own application. There was a philosopher a long time ago named Ludwig Wittgenstein who stated that principal—no rule determines its own application. This can be applied, and invoked, by anybody who wants to sue.

It is not going to be established that a country was not involved in aiding and abetting terrorism unless and until a complaint is filed, discovery is engaged in, the country's diplomatic and national security matters are probed into in a United States court, and they are subjected to all the processes of discovery in a United States court that, frankly, interfere with the ability of this country to conduct its foreign relations, and terrify foreign governments, and I think justly. That is the problem.

Mr. FRANKS. So, Mr. Klingler, I will turn to you, sir. Recently, Bloomberg editorialized that in the event that foreign Nations respond to an enactment of JASTA by passing reciprocal measures of their own, ''The entirety of U.S. foreign policy could be put on trial in foreign courts under the guise of seeking monetary justice.'' Now, do you think this is a potential result of the enactment of JASTA? If not, what are your assurances that you might state? That microphone, sir.

Mr. KLINGLER. Thank you very much. Two principal reactions—one is the scope of JASTA itself. I mean, if the theory is that there is actual mirroring of JASTA's terms abroad, then the scope of our exposure arising from JASTA is limited to our undertaking acts of international terrorism. And the additional exposure of reciprocal retaliation would only be what JASTA extends beyond the current FSIA limitations.

In other words, a foreign state that is actually motivated and seeks to do that could do it today. They could say, ''The United States has Section 1605A. That allows a suit in our court based on a designation by the executive, and we designate the United States,'' they could do that. Or they could point to the tort exception, and say the United States Courts are divided over the scope of the tort exception, they all agree, and the State Department even agrees that acts of Americans abroad—or I am sorry—acts of a foreign state in America, would fall within the current exception. So we are going to extend or immunity exception to acts of Americans abroad.

So, JASTA itself contains a set of limitation, and does not extend current law particularly broadly. The other principal response, and I think what has driven this area for the last 40 years is that this is handled by the United States Government in an exceptionally professional and effective way. It is a political, military and diplomatic issue.

When a foreign country begins to restructure its judicial processes to direct their actions at the United States, we take a broad range of action. Judge Mukasey's point about Belgium, and our threatening to shift NATO, shows actually that we do have the capability to respond to this, that we can meet both sets of objectives. We can ensure that injuries in the United States can be redressed by our courts, and that inappropriate extensions of jurisdiction elsewhere can be met appropriately by our diplomatic forces. They have the tools to do that.

Mr. FRANKS. Professor Gurulé, some have argued that the enactment of JASTA will violate international law, as you know. Do you believe or do you not believe that the exception to foreign sovereign immunity included in JASTA will cause the United States to violate international law?

Mr. GURULÉ. No, I do not. I do not believe that it would violate international law, and the reason that I say that is that foreign sovereign immunity is not absolute, and we know that. An exception, again, has been highlighted in the Foreign Sovereign Immunities Act for torts committed within the United States.

Further, 1605A creates another exception, and foreign states have also recognized exceptions to foreign sovereign immunity for torts committed in their territory. So again, I do not believe that sovereign immunity is an absolute principal without exception. And other states besides the United States have recognized exceptions to foreign sovereign immunity.

Mr. FRANKS. Well, thank you. My time has expired, and I will now recognize the Ranking Member for 5 minutes.

Mr. COHEN. Mr. Klingler, let me ask you, how many clients do you have in this case?

Mr. KLINGLER. Very few. I represent an association of insurers. I work with co-council, who represent, you know, a much broader range. And at times, when I have, say, argued in the second circuit on this issue, it is on behalf of the broader range of plaintiffs.

Mr. COHENS. How many victims of 9/11 are involved?

Mr. KLINGLER. In the case generally, oh, the class action extends into, you know, the several hundreds.

Mr. COHEN. Did they not get compensated? Did they have to not except compensation to participate here?

Mr. KLINGLER. Certain of the victims have been compensated. The extent of the compensation, though, is quite limited. And even for the ones who were compensated, others have not been compensated at all. And even for the ones that have been compensated, both the extent of the injury, but particularly the process—the justice element—that what a number of the plaintiffs want more than anything else is an accounting. Someone to actually delve into the fact——

Mr. COHEN. I accept that, and the people that have not been compensated at all, is that because they are not direct victims or——

Mr. KLINGLER. Because they are not necessarily eligible under the particular compensation scheme. For example, for, you know, the massive property damage.

Mr. COHEN. All right, so it is property, not personal.

Mr. KLINGLER. Well, I think even some of the personal, but I am not familiar with how that line is drawn.

Mr. COHEN. Okay. Mr. Stephan, and I might have missed it in your address, but what is the harm, if you say that these people—foreign governments—will not appear; they just will not come to court jurisdiction just will not permit, and they will not pay off the judgement and it just kind of—so what is the harm in letting folks bring an action in court?

Mr. STEPHAN. Sir, the harm is, first, that you do not get the reckoning that people are looking for; you get no acknowledgement, you get no information.

Mr. COHEN. All right.

Mr. STEPHAN. Secondly, those default judgements, in turn, become problematic. We have talked about Iran; we have talked about legislation that this Congress has adopted that extended the scope of assets associated with Iran that might be used to pay off some of those judgments. Iran has initiated a claim in the International Court of Justice based on a treaty we have with them.

And it is possible—I am not saying it is likely—but it is possible that the United States will end up being on the hook for the money paid to Iran. We have seen something like that happen with our terrorism judgments supposedly collected against Cuba. So, there are consequences. It is not an empty gesture.

Mr. COHEN. Mr. Mukasey you talked about—I believe it was your statement—about other countries wanting to sue us—maybe it was Mr. Stephan—but that other folks want to sue us or bring action against us.

Mr. MUKASEY. It is not a question of suing us; it is a question of using this as a pretext, either for lawsuits, which would be, you know, one thing; but for other kinds of harassment of our people—military, diplomatic, and so on, it is a pretext, not that their going to enact identical legislation. That is not the way it works. They do things that interfere with our sovereign immunity, whether by harassing our diplomats or our soldiers. And then when we - - -

Mr. COHEN. But could they not do that now?

Mr. MUKASEY. They would not have the pretext of this statute that does not even depend on an executive determination of status as a foreign sponsor of terrorism. We are letting basically anybody walk into court and say, "We think this entity is a foreign sponsor of terrorism."

Mr. COHEN. I do not know that they need a pretext, but whatever. They have got all these problems abroad where we could be sued, and the drones we have killed at least a 100 people. Our litigation, we think, where there is a wrong, there is a remedy—in this case you are saying there is not a remedy, or are you saying this is the type of situation where mysteriously people appear and give somebody a bunch of money and do not say where it comes from, and then they leave?

Mr. MUKASEY. I am not sure I understand the question.

Mr. COHEN. Well, I understand that maybe it is nothing classified—it is something I read in the paper—that some of these victims of drone attacks, the heirs of the victims of drone attacks, somebody mysteriously shows up, gives them a whole bunch of money, and did they disappear. Is that the way we are supposed to remedy our errors?

Mr. MUKASEY. No.

Mr. COHEN. But we do that.

Mr. MUKASEY. Not necessarily, but if that is the reality of international relations then it is a whole lot better then airing our——

Mr. COHEN. Dirty laundry.

Mr. MUKASEY [continuing]. National security secrets in a tribunal overseas. Do I think it is desirable? No. Do I think it is better than the alternative?

Mr. COHEN. Let me get in my last question. You said something about Belgium, and there was a possible prosecution of Rumsfeld?

Mr. MUKASEY. Yes.

Mr. COHEN. What was that for?

Mr. MUKASEY. It was for war crimes.

Mr. COHEN. That makes me be more in favor of this. Thank you.

Mr. FRANKS. I now recognize the Ranking Member of the Committee, Mr. Conyers, for 5 minutes.

Mr. CONYERS. Thank you, sir, and I thank you for your testimony, gentlemen. Let me start with Mr. Stephan. Mr. Klingler and Professor Gurulé argue that concerns about reciprocal actions against our country in response to the enactment of this S. 2040 are overblown, noting that exceptions to sovereign immunity over the last 40 years have not resulted from a flood of litigation against the United States. What is your response, sir?

Mr. STEPHAN. Thank you for the question, congressman. My response is, first of all, until very recently, the tort exception in the Sovereign Immunities Act has been used for what Congress thought it was doing; cases like the Makharadze automobile accident here in D.C. 20 some years ago. It has not been used as a way of dealing with what are fundamentally national security issues, although also issues of justice.

As to the antiterrorism provision that we have had on the books for 20 years now, in essentially every case where claims have been brought, there has been retaliation by the countries involved. Our response is we do not care what Cuba does, we do not care what Iran does, and I suppose you could say that law does not ultimately matter one way or the other. Our power will get us where our power gets us.

But if you believe that law matters, I think changing our law in the way that is proposed by the Senate bill will have implications in the laws in other countries, and I think those legal changes will have consequences.

Mr. CONYERS. Thank you very much. Let me turn now to Mr. Klingler. Professor Stephan contends that the Justice Against Sponsors of Terrorism Act would allow a private litigant to leapfrog the political branches just to allege that a certain particular state sponsor, or sponsors of terrorism, based on the belief and hope rather than proof, leaving the decision of when to discard sovereign immunity to private litigants acting on incomplete information, and whose interests do not necessarily match those of our Nation as a whole. How do you respond to that, Mr. Klingler?

Mr. KLINGLER. Thank you very much. I think that rests on just a fundamental misunderstanding of how the Foreign Sovereign Immunities Act has been structured by the political branches.

Congress made the initial determinations, in both the tort exception and in 1605A, that there would be a series of judicial determinations related to—in the former case injury arising just in the United States; in the latter case, it would be injury arising anywhere subject to the executive determination. And what JASTA is seeking to do is really to restore that basic understanding that tort exception passed in 1976 by a political branch, that indicated that we do not want a politicized executive process to be the focus of determining when victims of a whole range of injures including terrorism, can get relief.

Instead, we will create narrow categories that are internationally recognized where the judiciary is the appropriate forum for that. That was the basic decision in 1976, and JASTA just carries that forth.

Mr. CONYERS. Professor Stephan, do you support that view?

Mr. STEPHAN. I would like to distinguish, sir, between the 1976 decision and the 1996 decision. As to the creation of the antiterrorism exception in 1996—and that was what I was referring to in my written remarks—that does require a separate judgment by the executive branch using criteria set out by this Congress. And what 1605(b) would do is eliminate that step. That was what I was referring to.

Mr. CONYERS. Ah. Well, would you have a final comment, sir?

Mr. KLINGLER. If I could. The 1605 executive power is preserved for all injuries overseas. And I think that we cannot underestimate the fact that there have been state-facilitated terrorism cases brought under the tort exception.

Let's go back decades—that is Liu in the ninth circuit, that is Letelier in the district court, and that is for the 9/11 cases apart from the Saudi case. Since 2008, the theory of JASTA is what underlies the claims against the Afghans that have been brought in the DDC and at least allowed to go into discovery by the Second Circuit.

Mr. CONYERS. Thank you sir, thank the Chair.

Mr. FRANKS. I thank the gentleman, and I now recognize Mr. Nadler for 5 minutes.

Mr. NADLER. Thank you. I think it was Mr. Klingler just mentioned the Letelier case. In the early 1970's, Orlando Letelier, the former Chilean Ambassador to the United States, was murdered in Washington, D.C. by operatives and senior officials of the Chilean Intelligence Services and two Cuban exiles. His survivors were permitted to sue the Chilean Government in American courts.

And the widow of Henry Liu, a Chinese journalist and critic of the Taiwanese Government, was permitted to sue Taiwan after her husband was murdered in California by agents of the former director of Taiwan's Defense Intelligence Bureau.

Yet that, I suppose I should ask Attorney General Mukasey, those cases did not resolve in any kind of retaliation or a flood of litigation against the United States. Why do you think that having JASTA restore the law as it was understood then, in this situation, would result in such retaliation?

Mr. MUKASEY. Because we are talking about far different scale, and a far different kind of involvement. Those were narrow acts focused on particular people, where a lawsuit took place on United States soil. This is something——

Mr. NADLER. The orders were given abroad.

Mr. MUKASEY. Understood, but this is something far different. The scale is far different, the alleged involvement is far different.

Mr. NADLER. Mr. Gurulé, would you answer the same question?

Mr. GURULÉ. Yeah, I disagree. I do not see the distinction. I think that, again, when a foreign state aids and abets a terrorist attack, whether it is against a single individual in the case of an assassination of Letelier, or a terrorist attack on a much larger scale, the foreign state should be held accountable for its criminal conduct. Second, the victims of the attack should be afforded a remedy, a judicial remedy. They should be afforded their opportunity to litigate the cause of action in court. And so I find that distinction——

Mr. NADLER. The essential question I am asking is not on the equities, which I think are clear—people ought to have a remedy. But, on the prudential question of if we were to enact this, would that not invite retaliation by foreign governments?

Mr. GURULÉ. I think, again, it is overstated, and I go back to the case involving the Islamic Republic of Iran. I mean it is been sued in the United States for acts of international terrorism that resulted in a large terrorist attack in Beirut, killing over 200 American servicemen. That litigation has been ongoing for over 10 years. It was brought to conclusion by U.S. Supreme Court——

Mr. NADLER. And this did not affect the JCPOA?

Mr. GURULÉ. There has not been a flood of litigation.

Mr. NADLER. Let me ask, Mr. Klingler Attorney, Attorney General Mukasey expressed concern in his testimony that enacting JASTA was almost certain to invite retaliation against our own government officials, soldiers, and diplomats in reference that the countries that would be most threatened by that would be the U.S., the U.K. and Israel in terms of individuals.

But JASTA only provides jurisdiction to sue foreign governments not individuals. And, if foreign governments were looking for an excuse to sue American Government officials, soldiers, and diplomats, would the existing tort exception not provide a sufficient excuse? First, Mr. Klingler, and then Attorney General Mukasey.

Mr. KLINGLER. You are absolutely right that JASTA does not apply to claims against individuals. The entire Foreign Sovereign Immunities Act does not apply to claims against individuals.

So, to the extent that there would be foreign governments that want to initiate jurisdiction to pursue individual Americans, that has nothing to do with reciprocating against either the Foreign Sovereign Immunities Act, or JASTA itself.

Mr. NADLER. So let me ask Attorney General Mukasey essentially the same question, but is your argument not really that any change to the—what is it, the Foreign Tort Act—even if it is a limited change, would give foreign governments the excuse to make bigger changes? And even if what we are doing would not evolve into claims against individuals, some foreign government might?

Mr. MUKASEY. That is a large part of it. I mean, one of the questions raised before was what if they passed legislation that mirrored what we are doing here? The issue is not mirror; the issue is caricature.

Mr. NADLER. So, your argument basically is that we should not make any change to the Foreign Sovereign Immunities Act, because it might lead to foreign governments to have an excuses to make worse changes?

Mr. MUKASEY. Only with a lot of hesitation and a lot of study, neither of which has been present here. This thing flew past the Senate with no hearings.

Mr. NADLER. Well we do not duplicate the Senate's practices.

Mr. MUKASEY. I understand that, and I commend you for it.

Mr. NADLER. Mr. Gurulé, my last question since my time is running out. There was reference to Americans being arrested in Rome, I think it was, and subject to prosecution. But was that not a case where the allegation was that American CIA agents had, without any color of authority, kidnapped someone off the streets of Rome, and shipped him off to Syria to be interrogated and tortured by the Hafez al-Assad regime, and what happened to that litigation? Do you know?

Mr. GURULÉ. As far as I know, I think it is still pending. You know there were criminal charges that were filed against the Americans, and efforts are being made to in Italy bring them to justice.

But again, I would go back to the point—if there is a hostile foreign government, a hostile foreign government does not need any pretext, does not need any excuse, to bring criminal charges against the United States or it is citizens. And this legislation is not going to change that one way or the other.

Mr. NADLER. My time has expired. Thank you very much.

Mr. FRANKS. I thank the gentlemen, and I now recognize Mr. Deutch for 5 minutes.

Mr. DEUTCH. Thank you Mr. Chairman. Judge Mukasey, I just want to go back to something you said earlier about the role that a court would actually play here. I mean, there is a terrorism exception currently, right, under the foreign sovereign immunities?

Mr. MUKASEY. There is terrorism exception when the United States Government has designated a foreign state as state sponsored terror.

Mr. DEUTCH. State sponsor of terror, right.

Mr. MUKASEY. So that takes care of the issue of who decides initially that this lawsuit should even go on, because——

Mr. DEUTCH. Right, right, I understand. And that is where I am going. So, when the proposed statute refers to a tortious act, a foreign state or its official employee agent acting within the scope of her office, regardless of whether the tortious conduct took place, that is what requires, I think as you suggested—and this is what I do not understand just from your years of experience—that is what you suggest requires a—before determining whether there is an exception, before knowing that the country was actively involved in terrorism, the only way—I guess you are suggesting the only way we are going to know that is if it is determined. And the only way to determine that under this statute would be in court.

Mr. MUKASEY. Correct.

Mr. DEUTCH. And how would you expect that would play out? That is what I am trying to get at.

Mr. MUKASEY. A complaint gets filed.

Mr. DEUTCH. Yeah.

Mr. MUKASEY. That complaint is judged solely on its four corners. In other words, do the allegations in the complaint allege a claim? Not is there any evidence to support the claim, et cetera. You then go through what is known fondly as discovery, which is an exercise that involves probing into the documents and the witnesses on each side. In a civil case, that is an unexceptional exercise.

When you are talking about litigating, with respect to the involvement of a foreign government, you are talking about subjecting their internal deliberations, their national security documents, their documents that may very well involve cooperation with the United States, to public scrutiny in a court, and it becomes a very different matter, and there are very different considerations. That can be done by anyone, regardless of whether it serves the interest of the United States or disserves them, and that is what I think is objectionable.

Mr. DEUTCH. Mr. Klingler, how do you respond to the suggestion that a case gets filed, and suddenly in discovery, there are requests for the production of all kinds of documents that might be used to show a connection that for a whole host of national security reasons, let alone the concern of retaliation that have been discussed, should not be part of an extensive court case?

Mr. KLINGLER. Right, a couple of points. I mean, one is that foreign sovereigns are in U.S. courts every day under the various exceptions. Some of those manners are extremely sensitive—a number of—both on the tort exception and expropriations, and some commercial matters. And judges have developed a whole range of doctrines, some of which are very favorable to foreign sovereigns to make sure that discovery, if it even takes place, is limited; that there is direct appeal in cases of the unnecessary invasion of the foreign interest.

And frankly, we should kind of keep in mind what the national security context is here. And judges manage this issue everyday. I do not have the experience obviously of Judge Mukasey, but the issue here is whether the state facilitated a terrorist attack on U.S. soil. That may implicate various correspondence, it may implicate various correspondence with other governments.

The United States has the ability to enter appearances and help to manage that issue, but the national security sensitivity is going to be whether the Nation attacked us or not, or facilitated those who did.

Mr. DEUTCH. Right. Mr. Stephan, right, so there is an argument that I think a lot of people would make just listening to this; understand we are concerned about what maybe brought out in court, but if what we are talking about bringing out in the course of litigation under this statute is an active role played by a foreign government in a terrorist attack, why would we not expect that to be the result?

Mr. STEPHAN. Congressman Deutch, let me play law professor, if you will allow me, and put before you a hypothetical. In many parts of the world——

Mr. DEUTCH. As long as I do not have to answer your question.

Mr. STEPHAN. Yes, sir, I will try to answer my own. In many parts of the world—not only in the Islamic world, but in Europe—it is believed that Israel is the real perpetrator of the 9/11 attacks. Suppose a victim of that attack files suit against Israel under this law.

Under the current bill as I see it, there is no barrier at which point discovery ensues, in which Israel will have to try and prove a negative; that in spite of its obvious interest in concealing under this—if I may so, paranoid account—but still one that is commonly believed. What is discovery going to look like, in that case? That, in a nutshell, is my concern.

Mr. DEUTCH. If I can just ask Professor Gurulé, so should we would be concerned that if we pass this, suddenly cases are going to be brought all over alleging the most outrageous things that ultimately would not just be outrageous, but would actually start to compromise our national security?

Mr. GURULÉ. Again, I think this is highly speculative. And anything is possible, but just because something is possible does not make it true, that it is going to happen. And the possibility that someone may seek to sue is real with respect to the 9/11 attacks, again is so highly unlikely, so speculative, that it does not undermine all of the good, all of the value, and the positive purposes, value that would be brought by enacting this legislation.

Mr. DEUTCH. Thanks. Mr. Chairman, I yield back. I thank the panel. This was very helpful, very instructive.

Mr. FRANKS. Well, this concludes today's hearing and, without objection, all Members will have 5 legislative days to summit additional written questions for the witnesses or additional materials for the record.

And I just want to especially thank the witnesses and the Members and the audience for being here today. I appreciate all of you taking the time to be here. And with that, this hearing is adjourned.

[Whereupon, at 11:56 a.m., the Subcommittee was adjourned subject to the call of the Chair.]

www.ingramcontent.com/pod-product-compliance
Lightning Source LLC
Chambersburg PA
CBHW081840280526
45789CB00007B/2517